AF673709

365 Tales Of Hanuman

Om Books International

Om Books International

Reprinted in 2025

Corporate & Editorial Office
A-12, Sector 64, Noida 201 301
Uttar Pradesh, India
Phone: +91 120 477 4100
Email: editorial@ombooks.com
Website: www.ombooksinternational.com

Sales Office
107, Ansari Road, Darya Ganj
New Delhi 110 002, India
Phone: +91 11 4000 9000
Email: sales@ombooks.com
Website: www.ombooks.com

Retold by Swayam Ganguly

ISBN: 978-93-52768-63-9

Printed in China

10 9 8 7 6 5 4 3

Contents

1 Shiva Curses Vishnu

Shiva was heartbroken at the death of his wife Sati. He flung the dead body of Sati on his shoulders and started doing the Tandava dance that threatened to destroy all the Three Worlds.

"Please pacify Lord Shiva," Sage Narada requested Vishnu. When Vishnu appeared before Shiva, he thought, *I will have to calm Lord Shiva down and do something to stop the Tandav.* Vishnu used his Sudarshan Chakra to cut Sati's dead body into eighteen parts, matching the sound of the chakra with the rhythm of Shiva's feet touching the ground. These pieces fell on Earth to form places of pilgrimage.

When Shiva realised what had happened, he cursed Vishnu angrily, "You shall be born on Earth and be separated from your wife, experiencing the same pain of separation as me." After Shiva calmed down he realised what he had done. "I cannot take back the curse," Shiva said to Vishnu, "But I shall help you share its pain. My incarnation on Earth shall serve yours and help you find your wife," he promised.

2 Shiva's Incarnation

Vishnu decided to be born as Rama to rid the Earth of its evil forces. His consort Lakshmi would be born as Sita. Shiva pondered over how he would help Rama on Earth. *If I take birth in the form of a human, I will not be able to serve Vishnu properly as he will also be born as a human*, Shiva thought. *A servant can never be equal to his master.*

After a lot of thought, Shiva decided to be born in the form of a powerful monkey. *A monkey is an honest and humble animal with simple needs and a simple lifestyle*, Shiva concluded.

Thus, Shiva was incarnated as Hanuman and played an important role in helping Rama vanquish Ravana and his evil forces. Rama was so pleased with Hanuman that he made him a Chiranjeevi. Hence, Hanuman is one of the seven immortals on Earth to be blessed with an everlasting life.

3 The Arrogant Ravana

Ravana was one of the greatest devotees of Lord Shiva with whose blessings he had defeated all his enemies. But power had made Ravana extremely arrogant. He thought, *Why don't I visit Lord Shiva and request him to come and live with me in Lanka? He cannot say 'no' to me as I am his greatest devotee*!

Ravana arrived in Kailash. "Inform Lord Shiva that I have come to meet him," he rudely said to Nandi.

"What do you want, Ravana?" Nandi asked. "The Lord is busy now."

"I want Lord Shiva to come and live with me in my kingdom Lanka," Ravana proudly stated. "That is why I have come to invite him and take him away with me."

"Have you lost your senses, Ravana? You are selfish and arrogant!" Nandi exclaimed. "You are also foolish! What makes you think that Lord Shiva will leave Mount Kailash?"

4 Nandi Curses Ravana

"Why should Lord Shiva leave Goddess Parvati and his ganas to live with you in Lanka?" Nandi demanded. Ravana felt insulted when he was stopped from meeting Lord Shiva.

"How dare you advise me?" he furiously exclaimed. "You are just a bull, and stupid like a monkey!"

"Yes, I am a humble animal," Nandi replied. "But here in Kailash, unlike in Lanka, Lord Shiva treats everyone equally."

"I'm surprised that Lord Shiva has appointed an animal like you, who is like a monkey, as his mount and the head of the ganas!" Ravana said angrily. Now, Nandi lost his temper. "You keep calling me a monkey," Nandi thundered. "I hereby curse you that a monkey shall pave the way for your downfall!"

Nandi's curse came true as the monkey god Hanuman was born as Shiva's incarnation. He helped Rama defeat and kill Ravana in battle.

5 Narada Desires to Marry

Two celestial sages Parvat and Narada once visited Ambarish, the ruler of Ayodhya with a desire to marry his beautiful daughter, Shrimati.

"As I asked you first, I should marry Shrimati," Parvat requested Ambarish.

"No. As I'm older and wiser than Parvat, I'm a more suitable groom for your daughter," Narada said.

"I request both of you sages to attend Shrimati's swayamvara where she will choose her groom herself," Ambarish requested the two sages. Narada immediately rushed to Lord Vishnu to seek his help.

"Please make me as beautiful as you, Hari, so that Shrimati chooses me as her groom," Narada requested Vishnu.

If Narada gets married, he will not perform his duties as a celestial sage and all his divine powers will vanish! Vishnu thought. So, he blessed Narada. "May you look like Hari!" But Hari was also the name of a monkey, and Vishnu had transformed Narada's face into a monkey's face.

6 Narada Curses Vishnu

Narada was eager to get married to Shrimati. He immediately rushed back to Earth without realising that he now resembled a monkey. When Shrimati saw Narada, she laughed loudly. So did the entire gathering.

Narada thought, *How could Lord Vishnu subject me to this kind of humiliation*? He went to Vaikuntha and cursed Lord Vishnu without listening to an explanation. "I curse you that you shall always have to take the help of monkeys to fulfill your tasks," Narada thundered.

Lord Vishnu explained to Narada how he would lose his divine powers if he got married.

"Oh, what have I done?" Narada exclaimed sadly. "In my anger, I have foolishly cursed the Lord himself!"

Vishnu replied, "I shall convert your curse into a boon. It shall lead to the birth of Hanuman during my incarnation as Rama. He shall help me put an end to the demon-king Ravana!"

7 Durvasa Curses Punjikasthala

Once, a serious discussion was taking place among the gods and sages in Lord Indra's court. Sage Durvasa, renowned for his short temper and cursing people at the slightest provocation, noticed that the celestial nymph Punjikasthala was moving to-and-fro during the meeting. "Be still!" Durvasa chided her. But Punjikasthala continued moving here and there, ignoring Durvasa's warning. A furious Durvasa cursed her to be born on Earth as a monkey.

"Please forgive me," Punjikasthala fell at Durvasa's feet. "Do not punish me so harshly." "I cannot withdraw my curse," Durvasa softened a little. "However, I can reduce its effect. You shall return to Heaven after giving birth to a mighty son!"

8 Indra Curses Punjikasthala

Punjikasthala the beautiful nymph in Indra's court was arrogant and very proud of her beauty. Indra wanted to marry her. But the vain Punjikasthala rejected his proposal when he expressed his feelings for her. "How can I marry someone who has a thousand eyes?" she said to Indra. "My husband should be the handsomest in all the Three Worlds." Indra cursed Punjikasthala, "You shall be born on Earth as a monkey named Anjana." Punjikasthala was stunned. Her friend, another nymph named Adrika protested against Indra's curse.

"How could you curse her because she refused to marry you?" she shouted at Indra, mocking him in the voice of a cat, which further enraged Indra. "Why don't you join your friend on Earth as well?" Indra said to Adrika angrily. "As you like cats so much, you shall be born as one!"

9 The Third Curse

Celestial nymphs loved roaming the skies. Once, as Punjikasthala was wandering in the sky, she spotted a monkey sage below on Earth. The sage sat below a tree in a cross-legged posture and was meditating so deeply that he did not notice the nymph. *How dare he not acknowledge my presence*? Punjikasthala thought, and threw stones and fruits at the sage. As a stone hit the sage on the head, his penance was broken. He opened his eyes and spotted Punjikasthala with a stone in her hand. She trembled as the sage bristled with rage. "Why did you throw stones at me?" the sage demanded. Punjikasthala was silent out of shame.

"Because you think my appearance is funny, I curse you to be a monkey!" the sage thundered.

10 Punjikasthala Prays to Lord Shiva

Punjikasthala pleaded with the monkey sage to take back the curse. "I cannot do that. Pray to Lord Shiva to bless you with a child and relieve the curse," he advised Punjikasthala. Soon, Punjikasthala noticed fur growing on her body. She rushed to a nearby river and was shocked to see her reflection in the water. She had the face of a monkey.

Suddenly, she recalled the monkey sage's advice. *I shall pray to Lord Shiva*! Punjikasthala thought. *Once, I am blessed with a child the curse shall be over and I can return to heaven. Henceforth, I shall be named as Anjana*. She created a small lingam of Lord Shiva and started praying to him in the forest. Her deep penance pleased Shiva. He summoned Vayu, the God of Wind. "I shall be reincarnated on Earth as Anjana's son," Lord Shiva informed Vayu. "You must help me."

11 Anjana and Kesari

Anjana found shelter in a hermitage in the forest which was terrorised by a demon named Sambasadan. *It's my duty to protect these kind sages for having offered me food and shelter*, Anjana thought. She prayed to Lord Shiva to seek his help.

"Sambasadan can be destroyed by no one but his own blood," a divine voice proclaimed to Anjana. As she went to battle Sambasadan, she was joined by the brave and powerful monkey-king Kesari. Together, the pair attacked Sambasadan. Anjana remembered the divine advice, and dipped her arrow in Sambasadan's blood and shot him. Each arrow weakened the demon. Then Kesari dipped his spear in the demon's blood and pierced his heart. Finally, Sambasadan was killed.

12 Anjana Marries Kesari

The people of the hermitage rejoiced after the death of Sambasadan and thanked Anjana and Kesari. The head of the sages told Anjana, "We reward all those who win a battle for us with something special." "I was just performing my duty," Anjana replied. "I do not need anything for my services."

"Together with Kesari, you have defeated the invincible Sambasadan," the sage explained. "That makes you the perfect life partners. Will you marry Kesari? Kesari is more than willing." Anjana hesitated. But she was attracted to the bravery and humility of Kesari and agreed. Kesari and Anjana were married by the sages on an auspicious day.

13 Dasharath's Wives Share the Pudding

Once, King Dasharath of Ayodhya was performing a yajna to have sons. Agni, the God of Fire, gave some divine pudding to Dasharath.

"Divide this pudding among your three wives," Agni instructed Dasharath. Dasharath gave the pudding to his queens Kaushalya and Kaikeyi. Just as he was about to hand it over to his third queen Sumitra, an eagle snatched the pudding and flew away.

This bird was actually an apsara named Suvarchala who had been cursed by Brahma to be born as an eagle. "You will be freed from the curse after you touch the pudding given by Agni to Dasharath," Brahma had told her. As soon as the eagle snatched the pudding from Sumitra's hands, she was transformed back to the form of Suvarchala.

"Take half of our share of the pudding," Kaushalya and Kaikeyi offered to Sumitra. Sumitra gave birth to two sons named Lakshmana and Shatrughna, having the double share of the pudding. Kaikeyi gave birth to Bharat and Kaushalya gave birth to Rama.

14 The Birth of Anjaneya

Sage Agastya visited Anjana and Kesari who received him with great hospitality. "Ask for a boon," Agastya said to Anjana, who asked for a mighty son.

"Pray to Lord Shiva on the Venkatadri Hills located on the banks of Akash Ganga," he instructed Anjana. Anjana followed Agastya's instruction and started her meditation.

Meanwhile, when Suvarchala regained her celestial form, the divine pudding she had stolen from Sumitra fell from her claws. Vayu, the god of wind blew the pudding to where Anjana was meditating and guided it onto her lap. He said "I'm pleased with your devotion. Soon, a son will be born to you who will be an incarnation of Lord Shiva and will match my powers of speed and strength." Then Vayu asked Anjana to eat the pudding. Soon, Anjana gave birth to a mighty son who was named Anjaneya. Later, he was named as Hanuman.

15 Anjaneya and Vayu

Born by the grace of Vayu, the god of wind, Anjaneya was also known as Pavanputra or Vayu's son. Vayu struck up a great bond of friendship with little Anjaneya.

"Catch them, Anjaneya!" Vayu would yell, and Anjaneya would run after the leaves and flowers as Vayu blew them across rivers, up the mountains and towards the heavens. In this way, Vayu trained Anjaneya for his role ahead in life.

When Anjana would find her little son missing, she would yell out for him. Anjaneya would then sit on an air cushion that Vayu made for him and float towards his mother.

16 Anjana Departs from Earth

After giving birth to Anjaneya, Anjana was freed of her curse. With a heavy heart, Anjana said goodbye to her son as she prepared to fly towards Heaven. "What if I feel hungry mother?" Anjaneya asked Anjana. "You may eat the fruits on the trees whenever you are hungry, Anjaneya," Anjana replied. "But there are so many fruits," a confused Anjaneya asked. "Which fruits should I eat, mother?" "Eat the fruit that is as bright as the rising sun," Anjana told her son. Then, she left for her heavenly abode, leaving Anjaneya in the care of Kesari. *Let me eat some fruit as Mother had told me to*, Anjaneya decided when he was hungry and stepped outside. He saw the rising sun and recalled his mother's words.

17 Anjaneya Scares Surya

When Anjaneya saw the bright red morning Sun, he mistook it for a ripe, juicy mango. He climbed on top of a nearby hill. Vayu gave him a gentle push and lo, Anjaneya was flying in the air. Soon he gathered speed and flew rapidly towards Surya.

An alarmed Surya exclaimed, "That little fellow is charging towards me like a mad bull!" Vayu was proud of Anjaneya to have instilled fear in the heart of Surya himself. Anjaneya had increased his speed now, opening his mouth wide to swallow Surya. This alarmed Surya and he cried out to Indra for help. "Save me!" Surya shouted. "An asura is arriving to gobble me up!"

18 Anjaneya Chases Rahu Away

As Anjaneya flew towards the Sun, he saw the large head of demon Rahu trying to swallow it. After the churning of the ocean, the demon Rahu had disguised himself as a god to drink the nectar of immortality. Surya had exposed his true identity and foiled his plan. Lord Vishnu then beheaded Rahu. To seek revenge against Surya, Rahu's head swallowed the Sun from time to time, thereby causing a solar eclipse.

Anjaneya did not know all this. He was just very angry when he saw someone else trying to eat his precious fruit. He forcefully pushed Rahu's head away from the Sun. Rahu's head fled from the scene at Anjaneya's onslaught.

19 Indra Is Worried

After being beaten up and chased away by Anjaneya, Rahu decided to complain to Indra who heard him with concern. Indra thought, *If this boy swallows the Sun, I shall be his next victim. He will replace me as Head of the Devas. I must put an end to him right now*!

Mounted on his elephant Airavat, Indra rushed to protect Surya. Anjaneya had by now almost reached Surya. "Stop, child!" Surya ordered Anjaneya. "Do not come any closer or you will get hurt!" *The fruit itself is asking me not to come any closer, he thought with wonder. Maybe it doesn't want me to eat it. But eat it I shall*! Anjaneya sped towards the frightened Surya even though the scorching heat burned his body. Surya was stunned to see that his blazing heat had no effect on Anjaneya.

20 Indra Attacks Anjaneya

By the time Anjaneya was really close to the Sun, Indra also reached there mounted on his tremendously powerful elephant, Airavata. Forgetting all about his hunger Anjaneya grabbed Airavata by the tusks and rendered him totally helpless. Indra released his powerful Vajra or the thunderbolt which struck Anjaneya's face with full force, rendering him unconscious. He floated back to Earth slowly like a feather as Surya, Indra and Airavata sighed in relief.

Vayu rushed to gather the falling, now lifeless, child in his arms. Vayu then flew into a cave, swearing revenge against Indra who had harmed Anjaneya. "I shall punish anyone who worships Indra," Vayu vowed.

21 Vayu's Rage

Vayu was devastated to see that Anjaneya had been killed by Indra. Then, his sorrow turned to anger and he locked himself in a cave with his dead son. He withdrew all the air from the Universe and kept it with himself.

The world was suddenly thrown into a state of panic and chaos.

"Oh, I can't breathe!" Gods, demons, people, animals and plants exclaimed in unison. When Brahma saw that his creation was about to end, he rushed with a deva to where Vayu was hiding in the cave.

He discovered Vayu shedding tears beside the dead body of Anjaneya.

"What's the matter?" Brahma asked Vayu worriedly. "Why have you stopped performing your duties?"

"My Lord, go and ask Indra the reason," Vayu exclaimed angrily.

"He has killed my child Anjaneya!"

22 Brahma Mediates

Vayu was angry with Brahma on being asked why he had failed to do his duty. After Vayu told Brahma what Indra had done, Brahma became angry as well. He summoned Indra immediately. After Indra arrived, Vayu turned to him angrily.

"You are a coward!" he accused Indra. "How could you attack my defenceless child with your vajra?"

"Your son was about to swallow the Sun. I had to stop him," Indra explained.

Brahma scolded, "Every time you are scared, you start using your Vajra.This time you used it on a child!"

"Please forgive me," Indra said with folded hands to Brahma and Vayu.

"What good is an apology?" Vayu shouted. "Will it bring my dead child to life?"

"I shall bring Anjaneya back to life," Brahma promised.

23 Anjaneya Named Hanuman

Brahma took some water from his kamandalam or holy jug. He sprinkled some water on Anjaneya's lifeless body and uttered some mantras. Then, he touched the child on his chin. To Vayu's surprise, Anjaneya was revived instantly as if he had woken up from a deep sleep. He stared at the three gods in amazement. Vayu happily hugged his son.

"What's this mark on Anjaneya's chin?" Vayu exclaimed. There was a deep injury mark on Anjaneya's chin.

"That's the mark of Indra's thunderbolt," Brahma explained. "I'm afraid that cannot be rectified, and Anjaneya will have to live with that mark forever."

Vayu did not mind that. A son who was alive was much better even if he had a broken jaw. As Anjaneya felt his broken chin, Brahma announced, "Henceforth, you shall be known as Hanuman or 'the one with the broken chin'."

"Please release the air," Brahma requested Vayu who obliged immediately.

24 The Gods Bless Hanuman

Anjaneya was renamed Hanuman and all the gods in Heaven blessed him in the form of a divine light

"Son, I am sorry for having injured you," Indra apologised. "To make up for my mistake, I shall grant you a powerful boon - You will die only when you wish to die! Also, no weapon will be able to wound or hurt you."

Lord Brahma now stepped forward. "The Brahmastra is one of the most powerful weapons on Earth. I grant you complete immunity from that, my child. If the Brahmastra is used against you, you will never be affected by it. You will also live as long as I do."

"Hanuman, may you live all your life serving God and be regarded as the greatest devotee ever!" Lord Vishnu proclaimed. "You will have superhuman strength surpassing even Garuda!"

"You shall never be affected by fire," Agni promised.

"May you be blessed with speed mightier than the fastest wind," Vayu blessed Hanuman. Thanks to the boons received from the gods, Hanuman became superhuman and immortal.

25 Hanuman Acquires Siddhis

After Brahma, Indra and Vayu had blessed Hanuman, Surya blessed him with radiance, brilliance and the knowledge of the arts and sciences. Surya also granted two special Siddhis to Hanuman - the Mahima Siddhi and the Laghima Siddhi. The Mahima Siddhi helped Hanuman to transform into a gigantic size and the Laghima Siddhi helped him transform into the tiniest creature.

"You shall always be safe in and from water," Varuna the god of the ocean blessed Hanuman.

"May you lead a healthy life free from any curse or illness," Yama the god of death said. The god of wealth Kubera blessed Hanuman with eternal happiness.

"No objects or weapons can harm you," Vishwakarma, the divine architect blessed Hanuman.

Last but not least, Lord Shiva arrived and gifted his incarnation a kavach or a band that would keep Hanuman safe forever. With all the blessings and boons that the young and innocent Anjaneya received, he became the mighty Hanuman who struck terror in the hearts of his enemies.

26 The Mischievous Hanuman

Although Hanuman had been blessed with many boons by the gods, he was after all, just like any other innocent and curious boy of his age. He was very naughty and his mischiefs were causing problems for everyone specially since he had been blessed with supernatural powers. As Hanuman grew older, his pranks increased. No one, not even his father Kesari could control him as he roamed fearlessly in the forests all day.

"I challenge you to a fight," Hanuman would call out to fearsome tigers, lions and wild elephants. These wild animals were no match for Hanuman and fled at the mere sight of him. Hanuman would catch them by their tail, swing them in the air and throw them in the distance. When he was a child, everyone found his antics amusing. But when Hanuman grew up, he turned destructive. He teased the animals. He would swing on the trunks of the elephants when he was bored of swinging from trees. He also caused the destruction of the forest by uprooting trees.

27 Hanuman Troubles the Sages

Hanuman became more mischievous because of his supernatural powers. No one dared to punish him. A bold Hanuman began troubling the pious sages who used to pray in the forest.

Hanuman would pull the beard of one meditating sage and scratch the back of another or drench a third one in water. The sages would sometimes be frightened by weird animal noises that Hanuman made to disturb their meditation. Sometimes, Hanuman would climb up a tree and pelt the visitors to the sages' hermitage with fruits to make them run away. Once, as the sages performed an important holy ritual, Hanuman climbed up a tree and doused the sacrificial flame with coconut water.

"Ha ha!" Hanuman laughed as the sages glared at him angrily. The sages were peace-loving and had so far tolerated Hanuman's pranks with great patience. But this time, they were greatly angered as their holy ritual was disturbed.

"This naughty monkey must be taught a lesson," they exclaimed. "Let's complain to Lord Brahma."

28 The Sages Complain to Brahma

The sages were tired of Hanuman's endless pranks and mischief. They approached Lord Brahma as they were powerless to defend themselves.

"O Lord," they addressed Brahma with folded hands. "Hanuman has made our lives miserable. Please do something about him. Please help us."

"What has Hanuman done?" Lord Brahma asked worriedly.

"We never get a moment's peace because of Hanuman," the sages complained angrily. "He disturbs us whenever we sit down to meditate and chases away our followers, denying us food and alms. The animals in the forest are terrified of Hanuman who treats them cruelly. Today, Hanuman crossed all limits as he disrupted an important ritual by throwing coconut water on the sacrificial fire."

Hanuman is wasting his powers and hidden talent by engaging in such mischief. He doesn't realise that he has been born on Earth for a special purpose. He has to play an important role by assisting Lord Rama in defeating Ravana and his evil forces. I must help him so that he uses his energy in the right direction, Lord Brahma thought.

29 Brahma's Mild Curse

"Don't worry!" Lord Brahma assured the sages. "I shall teach Hanuman a lesson!" *I cannot take away the boons that have been bestowed on Hanuman*, Lord Brahma thought. *I shall calm him down using other means.* He placed a mild curse on Hanuman.

"Hanuman, for now you shall forget all the special powers that have been bestowed upon you. But when needed, someone close will help you recollect and use these powers for the benefit of mankind," he said. The curse transformed Hanuman, who gave up all his mischievous activities. He solely concentrated on meditation and studies, delighting the sages in the forest. He remained blissfully unaware of his superhuman powers till Jambavan, the king of the bears reminded him that he was capable of flying over the ocean to Lanka in a single leap.

30 Hanuman's Education

Lord Brahma's mild curse sobered Hanuman and he now focussed on acquiring knowledge. "Son, there is no better teacher than Surya, the most learned deva in this Universe." Kesari told Hanuman. "But how do I approach him?" a surprised Hanuman asked. Lord Brahma's curse had made him forget about his supernatural powers. Kesari reminded him how once he had flown towards the Sun to swallow it, mistaking it to be a ripe fruit. Thus reminded, Hanuman flew towards Surya who was alarmed when he saw Hanuman flying towards him. But Hanuman greeted him, revealing the purpose of his visit. "My Lord," Hanuman said bowing before Surya. "I'm Hanuman, the son of Anjana and Kesari. My father has advised me to become your student."

31 Hanuman's Idea

"O great Surya, "You know everything that there is to know. Please accept me as your pupil." Hanuman requested Surya. But Surya refused to teach Hanuman. "Son, I don't have the time to teach you. All day I am constantly riding across the sky. Where's the time to teach you?"

Hanuman was determined to learn from Surya. He was struck by a sudden idea. "My Lord, what if I face you and move backwards with you as you move during the day?" Hanuman suggested. "I shall fly at your pace before your chariot as you teach me."

32 Hanuman as Surya's Disciple

What dedication, determination and zeal this young boy has, Surya thought, impressed with Hanuman's unique idea. He agreed to be his Guru. "I shall teach you as I ride across the sky during the day. You shall fly backwards, before my chariot, facing me from dawn to dusk."

Hanuman flew before Surya's chariot despite the great heat and began his education. Due to the boons of the devas, he possessed a sharp mind. Soon, he mastered all the holy texts, the darshanas or the six systems of philosophies, the kalas or the sixty-four arts and the one hundred and eight occult mysteries of the Tantras. Hanuman proved to be more than a worthy pupil of Surya.

33 Surya's Proposal

Since he had vowed 'Aajanma Brahmacharya' (Bachelorhood), Hanuman was not eligible to study the Nava Vyakarnas (Nine Grammars). "You will have to marry to complete your education," Surya stated.

Hanuman was hesitant. Surya comforted him, "This marriage shall be temporary. Your divine wife Suvarchala will be created out of my rays and you will live separately after marriage which will only be for the welfare of the Universe. It will not affect your chosen path of celibacy."

34 Hanuman's Marriage

Hanuman reluctantly agreed to Brahma's proposal. A beautiful maiden named Suvarchala was created from Surya's divine rays. Hanuman married her. "Devotion shall be your eternal pursuit," Surya assured him. "Since you are going to be a Brahma in future, Suvarchala will take the place of Vani."

Hanuman lived apart from his divine wife, remaining a bachelor all his life. He completed the final part of his education by mastering the Nine Vyakarnas.

35 Hanuman's Gurudakshina

Hanuman had mastered all that he had set out to learn. Now as per custom, he had to pay for his education in the form of Gurudakshina to Surya. Hanuman addressed Surya, "You have taught me my responsibilities and the paths of virtue, honesty and devotion. What can I offer you as my Gurudakshina?"

Surya said, "Look after my son Sugreev, the younger brother of Vali, in the land of Kishkindha."

Hanuman promised to protect Sugreev always and returned to Earth in one mighty jump.

36 Hanuman Meets Shani

Surya also asked Hanuman to bring his wayward son Shani back on the right track. Hanuman agreed to attend to the matter at once and set off for Shanilok. He warned Shani to mend his ways. Shani was stunned at Hanuman's audacity. He shouted in rage, "I am Shani the invincible. Leave at once before I destroy you!"

Hanuman smiled and replied, "I have come to take you away with me to your father, Lord Surya. I shall not leave here without you!"

37 Hanuman Fights Shani

When Hanuman arrived at Shanilok to take Shani away to his father Surya, Shani was furious. He released flames to burn Hanuman. But all the flames got extinguished as soon as they hit Hanuman's body. Shani released weapon after weapon but none hurt Hanuman.

"Are you finished? Now, let us go as my Guru Lord Surya is waiting," Hanuman said calmly.

Shani attacked Hanuman angrily but fell on the floor after one resounding blow. Now, a desperate Shani jumped on Hanuman's head and started raining blows. Hanuman used his power of Mahima Siddhi to increase his size. As Hanuman grew in size and his head almost touched the ceiling, Shani was stuck between the ceiling and Hanuman's head.

"Oh!" Shani exclaimed. "Please set me free. I accept defeat!"

"Do you promise to mend your evil ways?" Hanuman asked.

"Yes, I do," Shani exclaimed.

"You must never harass my devotees," Hanuman stated.

"I promise never to trouble those who pray to you," Shani declared. Hanuman then took Shani to Surya who was overjoyed.

38 Hanuman and the Sage

Now that Hanuman had realised his supernatural powers again, he was back to his old pranks. *I must make Hanuman forget his powers again*! Lord Brahma thought.

One day, Hanuman was playing with an elephant and a tiger in the forest. Hanuman held the tiger by its tail and the elephant by its tusk. After revolving them in the air for some time, Hanuman got bored. Then, Hanuman saw a sage meditating in his ashram.

Let me have some fun! Hanuman thought. *I've heard that this sage is famous for his self-control and patience. Let me test him*!

Hanuman tied the tiger's tail to the elephant's tusk securely and left them outside the sage's hut.

When the sage tried to go for a bath in the river, the tiger outside his hut growled at him fiercely and the elephant stamped his feet angrily. The sage was so frightened that he rushed back into his hut while Hanuman had a good laugh.

When I find out the person responsible for this act, I shall teach him a lesson, the sage vowed.

39 The Sage Curses Hanuman

The sage ran to his hut as he saw a ferocious tiger and an angry elephant outside tied together.

How do I go for my bath to the river now? the sage thought worriedly. As he peeped out of the hut through the window, he saw Hanuman standing behind a tree.

"Come here, Hanuman!" the sage thundered.

Oops! Hanuman thought. *The sage is angry*! *I better obey him*!

The sage ordered Hanuman to release the animals. The tiger and the elephant ran away to the jungle as soon as Hanuman set them free.

"I hereby curse you that you forget all your powers," the sage said to Hanuman. Lord Brahma had made the sage curse Hanuman thus.

"Oh, why did you curse me like this?" Hanuman said, and started crying.

"I have cursed you for your own good, Hanuman," the sage replied. "This will help you control your strength and put it to good use for the Lord's service when the time is right!"

40 The Divine Monkey Trainer

Rama was an incarnation of Lord Vishnu on Earth. Lord Shiva desired to see the child Rama.

"Why don't you take Hanuman with you as well?" Parvati suggested.

"That's a good idea," Lord Shiva stated. "I'll take Hanuman with me when I go and see Rama. I shall disguise myself as a monkey trainer when I visit the court of King Dasharath in Ayodhya."

Lord Shiva visited Kesari.

"I would like to take Hanuman with me for a trip to Ayodhya for a few days," he requested Kesari who agreed readily. Hanuman was delighted to accompany Lord Shiva, and throughout the journey he kept on repeating, "He and I are one!"

Disguised as a monkey trainer and performing monkey, Lord Shiva and Hanuman arrived in Ayodhya. They started a monkey show on the streets. The people were delighted as they had never seen such a performance before.

"What great tricks this monkey is performing!" they exclaimed happily as Hanuman did somersaults in the air, danced and jumped through rings of fire.

41 Shiva and Hanuman Enter the Palace

When Lord Shiva and Hanuman tried to enter the palace of King Dasharatha, they were denied entry by the guards.

Lord Shiva was desperate to see Rama. He took out his divine drum and started beating it and Hanuman started dancing. As the sound of the drumbeats reached the interiors of the palace, the princes grew restless. The monkey trainer was ushered inside to perform before them.

Sage Vashishtha who had divine powers recognised Lord Shiva and bowed to him respectfully.

42 Hanuman Meets Rama

The four little princes Rama, Lakshmana, Bharat and Shatrughna were delighted to see the tricks of the monkey trainer. Rama fondly embraced the little monkey. When it was time for them to leave, he would not let the monkey go. The monkey trainer agreed to leave his monkey behind but refused to take any money.

"The value of this monkey cannot be measured in mere wealth. He is a fitting companion for the young prince of Ayodhya," he said. Only Sage Vashishtha who had recognised Lord Shiva realised the true meaning behind these words.

43 Rama Finds a Playmate

The monkey, Hanuman, became good friends with all the four princes of Ayodhya. He was loved by all of them. The four princes and Hanuman played together. Hanuman fetched their balls when they played in the field and held their kite strings when they flew their kites. When the princes swam in the waters of River Sarayu, the faithful Hanuman stood guard over them on the banks. When the princes practiced archery, Hanuman retrieved their arrows. Hanuman climbed trees and fetched fruit for the princes, especially juicy mangoes.

But Hanuman was especially close to Rama who grew so fond of him that he even started sharing his food with him. Hanuman became Rama's best friend. The bond of affection between them became stronger with each passing day.

One day, however, the moment of separation came suddenly with the arrival of Sage Vishwamitra.

"Send Rama with me to my hermitage to protect me from the demons who disturb me as I perform my yajnas," Sage Vishwamitra said to Dasharath.

"Wait for me at Kishkindha," Rama instructed Hanuman. "We shall meet soon!"

44 Hanuman Decides to Meet Narada

Kesari was aware that his son Hanuman was destined for greater things and would not stay with him for long now. Kesari decided to spend as much time as he could with him. One day, as father and son were sitting on the banks of a river together, they heard the sound of a very sweet musical instrument.

"What's that sound, father?" Hanuman asked.

"That's the sound of the Veena," Kesari replied.

"What is a Veena?" Hanuman asked.

"It's a musical instrument," Kesari replied. "I am sure that this is the sound of Lord Narada's Veena as no one else can play the Veena so sweetly."

"Who is Lord Narada?" Hanuman asked.

"He is Lord Brahma's son and a celestial sage. He's also one of the biggest devotees of Lord Vishnu. You must meet him to find out about his greatness," Kesari said.

"I shall meet him and be right back," Hanuman declared.

Before Kesari could stop him saying that this was not the way to meet someone like Narada, Hanuman was already flying away to meet him .

45 Hanuman Meets Narada

Hanuman followed the sound of the Veena and arrived where Narada was. "Who are you?" Narada asked, pretending he didn't know who Hanuman was. Hanuman greeted Narada respectfully. "I am Hanuman, O sage Narada," he said. "I have come to seek your blessings."

Narada said, "You have already received divine boons from the gods. What else do you want that you already do not possess?"

An adamant Hanuman replied, "I cannot think of anything right now but unless you bless me, I shall not leave from here."

"Well, the only thing lacking in you now is an aptitude for music," Narada said. "I hereby bless you that you will be an expert in music."

46 Hanuman's Song

Narada blessed Hanuman that he would be an expert in music. He was about to leave, when Hanuman stopped him. "Wait a minute," Hanuman said. "How will I know that I have become an expert in music?" Narada put his Veena upon a rock and sat down on the ground. "Sing a tune, Hanuman," he ordered. Hanuman began to sing. Soon, the rock on which Narada had kept his Veena began to melt. Narada saw his precious Veena floating in the liquid rock.

"Oh, stop!" Narada ordered. As soon as Hanuman stopped singing, Narada's Veena got stuck in the liquid rock. Narada was shocked. "Look what you've done, Hanuman," Narada exclaimed. "Sing the same tune again so that the rock melts once more for me to take my Veena out of it." But Hanuman got up and ran into his house. "Stop, Hanuman," Narada shouted as he ran after Hanuman.

47 Hanuman Tricks Narada

As Narada chased Hanuman, he entered Kesari's palace. Kesari discovered Narada panting for breath. "What is the matter, O noble sage?" he asked Narada. "Your naughty son, Hanuman has trapped my Veena in liquid rock and now refuses to release it," Narada exclaimed angrily.

"Hanuman, what are you doing?" Kesari asked firmly.

"Father, it was the only way to make Sage Narada bless each room of our palace by putting his holy feet inside," Hanuman explained. Both Narada and Kesari burst out laughing at this explanation. "Release Sage Narada's Veena immediately and bring it here," Kesari ordered Hanuman. After Hanuman handed over the Veena to Narada, the sage said, "Hanuman, you don't need my blessings. You are already blessed as you are Lord Rama's eternal servant."

48 Vali and Sugreev's Birth

Kesari instructed Hanuman that it was time for him to serve Vali, the king of the monkeys in Kishkindha. Suryadev has instructed me to serve his son, Sugreev. Although I shall serve Vali, I shall be Sugreev's follower, Hanuman decided.

"How did Sugreev become Lord Surya's son?" Hanuman curiously asked his father.

"Riksha was the monkey king before Vali," Kesari explained. "Once, Riksha fell into an enchanted pool and turned into a beautiful woman. Both Indra and Surya fell in love with her and she bore each a son. Indra's son was Vali and Surya's son was Sugreev."

49 Hanuman Leaves for Kishkindha

Hanuman was spellbound when he heard the story of Vali and Sugreev's birth. "What happened to Riksha after that? Who became the king?" Hanuman asked Kesari.

"Riksha regained his male form after bearing two mighty sons," Kesari explained. "He was the king of the monkeys and both the father and mother of Vali and Sugreev." Hanuman now wanted to know how Vali became king of the monkeys.

"After Riksha died, there was a power struggle between the monkeys as per the law of the jungle," Kesari explained. "Vali killed or maimed every other contender to the throne and became the undisputed ruler of the monkeys. But Vali is fond of his younger brother Sugreev and consults him in all matters."

"Then why did Lord Surya ask me to look after Sugreev and protect him?" Hanuman was puzzled.

"Tomorrow we shall travel to Kishkindha," Kesari told Hanuman. "I shall introduce you to King Vali and request him to take you under his protection." Hanuman was sad to leave his home and his father Kesari, but he felt a growing excitement to visit Kishkindha and meet Sugreev.

50 Hanuman Meets Sugreev in Kishkindha

On reaching Kishkindha, Hanuman bowed before Vali. Kesari requested Vali to accept Hanuman in his ranks. "I have heard many stories about you, Hanuman," Vali said. "My brother Sugreev also speaks fondly of you.It will be my pleasure to have you with us."

Hanuman had first met Sugreev at Pampapur where his father Kesari had sent him to gain knowledge in politics. The two had become friends there. Sugreev too was delighted when Kesari arrived with Hanuman. Vali noticed Sugreev's affection for Hanuman and appointed Hanuman to look after Sugreev. The bond between Hanuman and Sugreev grew stronger in time and Sugreev relied on Hanuman for almost everything.

51 Sugreev Becomes King

A demon named Mayavi arrived at the gates of Kishkindha. "Vali, come and fight me," he shouted. "You have killed many of my brothers." Vali picked up his mace and rushed outside. Sugreev followed him. When Mayavi saw both the brothers running towards him, he turned and fled. Vali followed Mayavi to his cave.

Instructing Sugreev to stand guard outside the cave, Vali said, "If I don't come out after a day, assume that Mayavi has won. Cover the entrance of the cave and return home." Vali entered the cave and indulged in a fierce fight with Mayavi. When Vali did not return after a day, Sugreev thought he was dead. He covered the entrance of the cave with a huge boulder and returned sadly to Kishkindha. He became the king of Kishkindha as advised by the other monkeys and appointed Hanuman as his chief minister.

52 Vali Banishes Sugreev

Vali killed Mayavi after a long battle that lasted for many days. He tried to exit the cave, but found it blocked. Somehow, he returned to Kishkindha and saw that Sugreev had crowned himself king. Vaali shouted. "You tried to kill me so you could usurp my throne."

"But I thought you were dead," Sugreev protested.

"The one to kill Vali hasn't been born yet. I shall spare your life as you are my brother, but you are banished forever from my kingdom," Vali said in anger.

As Sugreev turned to leave, Hanuman said, "I shall come with you." "Anyone who joins Sugreev is banished too," Vali thundered. Sugreev, Hanuman and a few of Sugreev's followers left Kishkindha.

53 Hanuman's Pledge to Sugreev

The cruel Vali did not allow Sugreev's wife and son to accompany him as he banished him from his kingdom. He forcibly kept them back in his kingdom and this act upset Sugreev a lot.

"Have patience, Sugreev," Hanuman comforted his friend. "Vali will soon realise that he has committed a great mistake by not trusting a brother like you."

"Oh, Hanuman!" Sugreev cried. "I have been banished from my land without any fault of mine. Why did Vali separate me from my family?"

"The truth will come to light sooner or later, my friend," Hanuman replied. "Have faith in God as everything happens for a reason."

"I have more faith in you than anyone else, Hanuman," Sugreev replied. "Please advise me where we should go now as I am sure Vali will try to kill me." Hanuman recalled his promise made to the Sun God of protecting Sugreev always. "As long as I am alive, Sugreev," Hanuman thundered, "Know this that not even Yamraj, the God of Death can touch you!"

The earth trembled and the mountains shook as Hanuman made this pledge. Sugreev embraced Hanuman warmly as the Sun smiled above. "Long live Hanuman," the monkeys cheered loudly.

54 Vali Torments Sugreev

After Sugreev was banished from Kishkindha by Vali, Hanuman suggested that Sugreev and his followers should go to Mount Rishyamukh.

"Vali cannot enter Mount Rishyamukh. He has been cursed by a sage that he will die if he enters Mount Rishyamukh," Hanuman explained.

Sugreev agreed happily as he was in perpetual fear of being killed by Vali. Any place where Vali could not come for fear of death seemed like Heaven to Sugreev. But Vali still wanted to humiliate Sugreev despite having banished him. After getting reports from his spies that Sugreev was hiding in Mount Rishyamukh, Vali decided to teach him a lesson.

Every day, Vali bathed in the ocean close to Mount Rishyamukh. He would fly low near Mount Rishyamukh and kick Sugreev hard on the head while he was praying. Then, Vali would fly away.

"Vali will not let me live in peace here," Sugreev complained to Hanuman after Vali had tortured him like this for a few days.

"Don't worry," Hanuman assured Sugreev. "I shall take care of Vali."

55 Hanuman Chastises Vali

The next day, as Vali flew low to kick Sugreev, Hanuman grabbed him mid air. "Release me at once. I am your king," Vali shouted as he struggled to break free. Hanuman paid no heed as he dragged Vali downwards towards Mount Rishyamukh.

"Hanuman, I shall die if I land there," Vali pleaded. "Promise me you shall never bother Sugreev again or I shall drag you down to your death."

"I promise," Vali said. "Now please let me go." Hanuman released Vali when they were inches away from the ground. *I'll teach Hanuman a lesson*, Vali thought as he flew away.

56 Vali Provokes Hanuman

Hanuman had finally humbled Vali who sought revenge against Hanuman. One day, when Hanuman was busy meditating in the forest, Vali reached there and disturbed Hanuman's penance. Vali mocked Hanuman, "Is your Lord Rama stronger than me? Can he beat me in a fight?" Hanuman ignored him. But Vali continued boasting loudly. Hanuman was irritated. "No one doubts your strength, O Vali," Hanuman stated calmly. "But why are you screaming about your prowess? Can't you see I am meditating?"

"I can defeat the one you are meditating to," Vali laughed mockingly and challenged Hanuman again.

57 Hanuman's Challenge

When Vali boasted that he could defeat Rama in battle, Hanuman was enraged. He challenged Vali to fight him. Lord Brahma thought, *Hanuman cannot kill Vali as only Lord Rama is destined to kill him. Hanuman's defeat will weaken Rama's forces in the fight against Ravana.* He told Hanuman to refrain from fighting Vali.

Hanuman replied, "I know that Lord Rama is destined to kill Vali. But as Vali has disrespected Lord Rama, I have no choice but to fight him."

58 Brahma's Advice

Hanuman was adamant to fight Vali despite Lord Brahma's dissuation.

"Vali has challenged Lord Rama himself and I have to answer his challenge." Brahma then reminded Hanuman of Vali's boon and advised him to take only a portion of his strength when he went to fight, and to surrender his remaining power at his altar of worship. Once the fight was over, he could return and regain his power.

Hanuman did as told and went to fight Vali. The Earth trembled and the gods gathered to witness this epic battle between Vayu's son and Indra's son.

59 Vali Is Humbled

As they faced each other, some of Hanuman's power shifted to Vali's body but soon Vali felt that the veins in his body would burst with so much power. Then, Lord Brahma appeared before him.

"Run away from Hanuman if you want to save your life," Lord Brahma whispered to Vali. "Keep running to drain the excess energy before it kills you."

Vali was brave but he wasn't a fool. *I must do as Lord Brahma says to save my life*, Vali thought, and ran away. He kept running non-stop for hours and felt a sense of relief after running for several miles. The excess energy in Vali's body got drained out. Suddenly, Vali saw Lord Brahma before him.

"You think you are the most powerful warrior," Brahma said to Vali. "But if Hanuman could do this to you with only one-tenth of his power, think about the consequences if he would have fought you with all his powers. Never make the mistake of challenging Hanuman again!"

60 Vali's Offer

Vali was humbled after Lord Brahma revealed to him how powerful Hanuman was. He started scheming some way to get Hanuman on his side. *With Hanuman as my general, my army will be invincible. I shall conquer the Three Worlds*, Vali thought.

"Please forgive me, Hanuman," Vali apologised to Hanuman. "I should not have provoked you by speaking ill of Lord Rama."

"Forget about it Vali," Hanuman replied. "I'm relieved I did not have to fight you."

Vali replied, "We are brothers. Remember the promise I made to your father about taking care of you? Join me to become my prime minister. Together, we shall rule the world. Abandon Sugreev!" Vali urged.

"You had told my father that we would be three brothers," Hanuman replied. "How can I abandon my other brother when I have taken a vow to protect him all my life? Please accept Sugreev back in your ranks. I shall join you after that." But Vali's pride did not allow him to accept Sugreev and he lost Hanuman's services as a result.

61 The Two Strangers

Because of a boon King Dasharath had given to his Queen Kaikeyi, Lord Rama was exiled from Ayodhya for fourteen years. Rama's wife Sita and brother Lakshmana accompanied him to the forest. In the forest, the demon king Ravana kidnapped Sita and took her on his flying chariot to Lanka. Rama and Lakshmana started searching for Sita and arrived at Mount Rishyamukh. Sugreev was terrified when he spotted the two armed brothers from a distance, wandering near the Pampa Lake.

"Hanuman, they must be Vali's spies," he exclaimed fearfully. "As Vali can't come here himself because of the curse, he has sent these two warriors to kill me."

"But they are men!" Hanuman replied doubtfully. "Why should Vali take the assistance of men to kill you?"

"Go in disguise and find out who those two men are," Sugreev ordered Hanuman. "If they are Vali's men as I suspect, send us a signal so that we may flee this place immediately. Go now, Hanuman!"

"Do not worry!" Hanuman assured Sugreev. "I shall immediately find out who these two strangers are."

62 Hanuman Meets Lord Rama

Hanuman disguised himself as a brahmin and approached Rama and Lakshmana. He didn't recognise them as he was a child when he had seen them last.

What a regal bearing these warriors have! Hanuman thought admiringly. *They cannot be ordinary mortals, and I think they are not Vali's spies. But who are they?*

"Who are you noble warriors disguised as ascetics?" Hanuman asked Rama and Lakshmana. "What brings you here?"

"We are here to meet Sugreev," Lakshmana replied. "But who are you to ask us such questions?"

"Please don't be offended," Hanuman replied. "As you have entered our land, it's my duty to ask you who you are. Sugreev himself has sent me here to find out your identities. Once you introduce yourselves to me, I shall escort you to Sugreev."

"I am Rama, eldest son of King Dasharath, and this is my brother Lakshmana," Rama replied. "We have arrived here to seek Sugreev's help as my wife Sita has been abducted by the demon king Ravana."

"Forgive me for not recognising you, My Lord," Hanuman said, revealing his true form.

63 Hanuman Narrates Sugreev's Story

Rama and Lakshmana were surprised to see the brahmin transform into a monkey. Introducing himself, Hanuman said with reverence, "I'm blessed to finally see you, My Lord. Forgive me for approaching you in disguise. Sugreev has been banished from his kingdom by his brother Vali. He lives in constant fear."

"How could Vali mete out such treatment to his younger brother?" Lakshmana thundered. "I would have killed him had I been Sugreev's friend." "Sugreev must be very sad to be banished from his kingdom and separated from his wife and son," Rama stated. "But he's also lucky to have a minister like you, Hanuman." Hanuman was over the moon to hear such praise from Lord Rama.

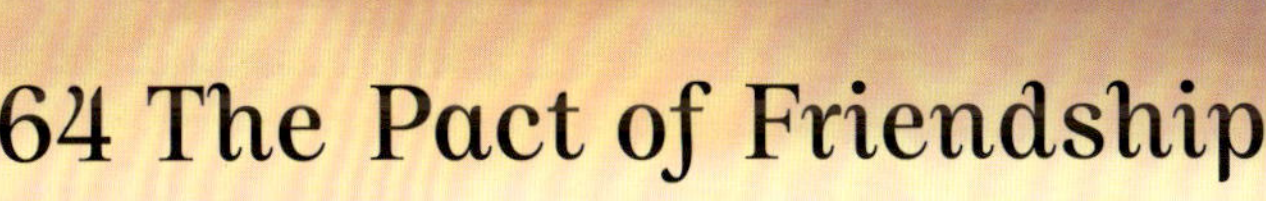

64 The Pact of Friendship

Hanuman bowed to Rama. "Sugreev will be happy to help you, My Lord," he said. "Like you, he is also in exile because of the cruelty of Vali. Sugreev will make a pact of friendship with you." "Please lead us to Sugreev, Hanuman," Rama requested. Hanuman assumed a gigantic form and bent down. "Please climb on my shoulders," he requested Rama and Lakshmana. He then held them and took a mighty leap to arrive at Mount Rishyamukh where he introduced Rama and Lakshmana to Sugreev.

"I am indeed fortunate that you seek my help and friendship," Sugreev said to Rama after hearing his story. With Agni (fire)as their witness, Rama and Sugreev then joined hands over the fire to seal their eternal friendship.

65 Sita's Ornaments

After the pact of friendship was sealed between them, Rama turned to Sugreev. "Sugreev, I shall help you regain your kingdom," Rama promised.

"O Lord Rama, I promise to help you find your wife Sita regardless of wherever she is hidden in Heaven or the Netherworld," Sugreev vowed. "I think we saw Sita being carried away by a demon. Now, I realise it was Ravana flying away with her on the Pushpaka Viman. She was crying out your name from the chariot and even threw down some of her jewels in a bundle below to us."

"Oh, where are they?" Rama exclaimed. "Bring them quickly to me, my friend."

"Don't worry. We have preserved her jewels safely," Sugreev replied, and ordered a monkey to fetch the jewels. Sugreev handed over Sita's jewels to Rama after they were fetched. Rama took them gently and was moved to tears.

"Oh Sita," he exclaimed. Hanuman was enraged to see Lord Rama in such pain.

I shall cause great suffering to that demon Ravana who has caused my Lord Rama so much pain, Hanuman pledged.

66 Rama's Plan

Rama and Lakshmana became emotional on seeing Sita's jewels. But Lakshmana was silent, as he felt himself responsible for having failed to protect Sita. "Oh Lakshmana don't you recognise Sita's jewels? Why are you quiet?" Rama asked.

"I don't recognise the bracelet and earrings, for I never saw her face. But I recognise the anklets that used to adorn her feet as I worshipped her feet alone," Lakshmana replied. Hanuman was struck by Lakshmana's devotion for Sita.

"We must find Sita Mata quickly," Hanuman opined. "But it's important to defeat Vali and place Sugreev on the throne to make our job easier. Once Sugreev has total command over all the apes, we shall gather a huge army." Everyone agreed with Hanuman's plan.

"But it is impossible to beat Vali in single-handed combat," Hanuman added. *Vali must be killed by treachery as there's no other way*! Rama thought. "Challenge Vali to a duel," Rama instructed Sugreev. "When the two of you are fighting, I shall shoot an arrow and kill Vali." Even though this method was unfair, no one protested as everybody wanted Vali to die.

67 Sugreev Challenges Vali

The next morning, Sugreev reached outside Kishkindha and shouted at Vali to challenge him.

"O Vali, come outside and fight me if you have the guts. You have banished me unfairly from my kingdom."

Vali was furious.

"It was my mistake to leave Sugreev alive," he exclaimed. "He dares to challenge me? I shall kill him."

Vali emerged from the gate of Kishkindha where Sugreev was waiting for him.

"Prepare for your death!" he shouted angrily at Sugreev.

"We shall see about that," Sugreev replied, confident that Lord Rama would kill Vali from his hiding place in the tree a little distance away from where the two warriors stood. Vali and Sugreev charged at each other and a fierce fight began. Rama aimed his arrow but was totally confused.

Both the brothers look exactly the same, Rama thought. *I cannot distinguish one from the other. I cannot shoot my arrow by guesswork as I might kill Sugreev by mistake.*

So, Rama was forced to hold his arrow. Sugreev in the meantime, was badly beaten up by his elder brother Vali.

68 Rama's Dilemma

Sugreev fought Vali bravely despite Vali having the upper hand in the battle. *Oh, I can't take this anymore*, a bruised Sugreev thought. *Why isn't Rama shooting his arrow?*

When Sugreev saw that Vali would surely kill him, he escaped.

"Come back you coward!" Vali shouted and chased Sugreev. But Vali gave up the chase when Sugreev entered Mount Rishyamukh.

"Oh Lord," Sugreev complained in agony later. "Why didn't you kill Vali as promised? If I hadn't been lucky enough to escape, Vali would have killed me. Why did you go back on your word? Rama was silent as Sugreev kept on talking angrily.

"Give Lord Rama a chance to speak, Sugreev," Hanuman said gently.

"Dear Sugreev," Rama said. "I didn't release my arrow as I was afraid of killing you by mistake."

"What do you mean?" a surprised Sugreev asked.

"Both you and Vali looked exactly the same when you were fighting each other in your bare bodies," Rama explained. "I simply couldn't make out who was who. Forgive me."

69 Hanuman Finds a Solution

Sugreev understood Rama's problem. "It's not your fault, Lord Rama," Hanuman said. "We should have told you about the strong resemblance between Vali and Sugreev. Saying this, Hanuman disappeared. He returned after some time carrying a garland of flowers and placed it around Sugreev's neck.

"You must challenge Vali to fight with him again," Hanuman told Sugreev. "This time, you shall be wearing this garland of flowers for Lord Rama to identify you." The very next day, Sugreev challenged Vali to a fight again wearing the garland of flowers. This time, Rama had no problem distinguishing between the brothers. Rama took careful aim at Vali and released his arrow. Rama's arrow found its mark and Vali fell dead on the ground. Rama crowned Sugreev the king of Kishkindha.

70 Hanuman Consoles Vali's Widow

After Vali's death, Hanuman visited Vali's grieving widow, Tara. Hanuman prostrated himself before her. "Oh, Hanuman! Why did my mighty husband have to die?" Tara sobbed.

"When he was about to die, I promised Vali that I shall take care of you and Angad," Hanuman replied. After a pause he added, "Lord Rama and Sugreev were only the means. Vali's own actions resulted in his death. Take refuge in Lord Rama who is Lord Vishnu's incarnation."

"Tell Sugreev that I have no ill feeling towards him. He had been wrongly banished by my husband," Tara said.

"Sugreev has asked for Angad to be crown prince of Kishkindha, instead of his own son," he informed her. Hanuman then told Tara that it was Vali's dying wish that Angad supports Lord Rama. "So it shall be," Tara replied.

71 Lakshmana's Anger

Many months passed by after Sugreev became the king of Kishkindha. Unfortunately, Sugreev drowned himself in worldly pleasures and completely forgot about the promise he had made to Rama about finding Sita. Meanwhile, Rama's restlessness grew day by day.

"Lakshmana, I think Sugreev should be reminded about his promise," he said. "Please have a word with Hanuman as he visits us every day."

Lakshmana conveyed the message to Hanuman, who immediately approached Sugreev.

"O king, it's time to fulfill your promise to Lord Rama," Hanuman reminded Sugreev.

"I shall look into the matter," Sugreev replied, and forgot about it again. After a few days, Lakshmana visited Sugreev.

"How dare you forget the promise you made to Rama?" Lakshmana asked Sugreev angrily. "It seems that you have forgotten everything after becoming the king. Don't forget that you owe your prosperity to Rama. If you don't fulfill your promise, I shall destroy your entire kingdom with my arrows."

Lakshmana's anger made Sugreev and his followers tremble with fear.

"Hanuman, please advise me what to do now," Sugreev pleaded nervously after Lakshmana left.

72 Hanuman's Wise Counsel

Sugreev asked for Hanuman's advice after Lakshmana threatened to destroy Kishkindha.

"My king, I had reminded you of your duty once," Hanuman said. "Fulfill your duty by helping Lord Rama. Apologise to him. You have failed to help Lord Rama after taking his help. Now, you must pacify him by doing what I told you," Hanuman stated.

Sugreev arrived before Lord Rama and said, "My Lord, I apologise for the delay in fulfilling my promise. I was just waiting for the rainy season to end so I could collect all my troops together."

"You should have shared your plans with us earlier," Lakshmana replied. "It would have spared the harsh words I said to you."

"You had every right to speak those words," Sugreev said humbly. "Between friends, one should not mind harsh words."

"What is your plan, Sugreev?" Rama asked gently.

"See, My Lord," Sugreev pointed at a huge force of monkeys gathered in the forest.

73 The Search Party

Rama and Lakshmana were impressed when they saw the huge force of monkeys.

"The plan is to divide my forces into four groups," Sugreev revealed. "Each force will go in each direction to look for Sita."

"That is a very good plan," Rama complimented Sugreev.

A pleased Sugreev continued, "Four great monkey leaders will be leading each group. But as Sita Mata is most likely to be located in the South, where Ravana's kingdom lies, I have equipped the fourth force with the strongest leaders."

"Who is in charge of the fourth group?" Lakshmana asked.

"The search team going southwards will have the mighty Hanuman, the crown prince Angad and the king of the bears Jambavan. As you are aware, the bears are our allies and have agreed to join us."

"That is good news," Rama exclaimed. "Such a search party led by three valiant heroes is bound to succeed."

"Please bless us so that we succeed in our mission," Hanuman declared as he, Angad and Jambavan bowed before him.

"May victory be yours," Rama blessed them happily.

74 A Frustrating Search

Of all the monkeys and bears in the search parties, Rama had the most faith in Hanuman.

"If there is anyone who can find Sita, it is you Hanuman," Rama said confidently to Hanuman before he set off with his search party. "Here, take my ring," he said, handing over his ring to Hanuman. "If you find Sita, it will be a sign to her that you are my messenger."

A determined Hanuman then set off southwards accompanied by Angad, Jambavan, and bears and monkeys of great strength and caliber. But even after a careful, extensive and lengthy search, the party found no trace of Sita.

"What shall we do?" the monkeys exclaimed. "Sugreev has given us only a month's time to find Sita. It's almost over."

After wandering far and wide, the monkeys grew totally exhausted. At last they arrived before the vast, roaring sea.

"The month's time to find Sita is over now," Angad declared to the search party. "We have failed!"

75 Hanuman Inspires the Monkeys

The southern search party was totally disheartened as the stipulated period set by Sugreev to find Sita was over. They sat down on the sea-shore sadly.

"What shall we do?" one of them asked Angad. "If we return empty-handed, King Sugreev is sure to punish us."

"We should fast to death," Angad suggested.

"What kind of talk is that, Angad?" Hanuman stated. "Giving up our lives just because we failed in our task is not a solution. We have tried our best, and there is no reason to think that King Sugreev will punish us because we have failed." But Hanuman's wise words went unheard. All the monkeys lay down on the sea-shore, ready to give up their lives. To inspire the monkeys, Hanuman began narrating the tale of Jatayu, who had sacrificed his life to save Sita.

"We should take some inspiration from the great Jatayu," Hanuman said. "He did not give up his life because he failed in his duty. He gave up his life to do his duty as a great devotee of Lord Rama."

76 Sampati Learns of Jatayu's Death

Sampati was an old vulture. He was unaware that his brother Jatayu had been killed by Ravana. From the cave where he lived, Sampati saw the group of monkeys.

Ah! Sampati thought, *One of these monkeys will make a nice meal.*

Sampati had a strong sense of smell, hearing and vision. He could gulp his prey at one go. He inched closer and as he was about to fly from a rock and swoop down, he heard his brother Jatayu's name mentioned several times by Hanuman.

"Be like Jatayu," Hanuman inspired the others. "If you wish to die, die fighting like him instead of giving up your lives for nothing. Despite his old age, see the bravery displayed by Jatayu in fighting Ravana to rescue Sita Mata. The brave bird would have succeeded if that treacherous demon hadn't cut off his wings."

After hearing Hanuman's narration about the heroic Jatayu, Sampati was shocked to learn about his brother's death.

77 Sampati Meets Hanuman

Sampati's appetite disappeared after he heard Hanuman talk about the death of his younger brother Jatayu. He flew down and landed before Hanuman.

"I am Sampati, the elder brother of Jatayu," Sampati introduced himself. "I overheard you talking about Jatayu and was curious. May I ask who you are and what you are doing here in this isolated land so far from your home?"

"I am Hanuman, the chief-minister of Sugreev, the king of the monkeys," Hanuman replied. "We have come here looking for Lord Rama's wife Sita Devi, who has been abducted by the wicked demon king Ravana."

"Is Jatayu really dead?" Sampati asked, and was heartbroken when Hanuman told him again how Jatayu had died fighting Ravana. Hanuman consoled Sampati.

"Lord Rama himself performed Jatayu's last rites and helped his soul attain salvation," Hanuman informed Sampati. "Because of his bravery and sacrifice, Jatayu has attained Heaven."

"Ravana shall pay for his evil deeds," Sampati said angrily. "I'm too old to fight him now but I'm sure that Lord Rama will do the job for me."

78 Sampati's Telescopic Vision

Sampati helped Hanuman and his group of monkeys by telling them the exact location of Sita.

"My brother Jatayu was a good friend of King Dasharath," he said to Hanuman. "He did his duty by trying to rescue Sita from Ravana. I must do my duty now. I had seen Ravana flying away on his chariot with a wailing woman across the ocean towards Lanka," Sampati revealed. "The woman was Sita as she was crying out Lord Rama's name."

"So, Sita Mata is in Lanka," a relieved Hanuman said as other monkeys rejoiced with relief.

"Let me check!" Sampati stated. Using his sharp telescopic vision, Sampati trained his eyes on the distant land of Lanka across the seas. This divine vision enabled Sampati to see faraway lands and objects with ease.

"I can see Lanka now," Sampati said to Hanuman and his friends. "Lanka is a city on Mount Trikoota located by the seashore. The city of Lanka is filled with lovely palaces, parks and gardens. I can see Sita now."

"Where? Where?" all the monkeys asked together.

79 Sampati's Valuable Information

Using his sharp telescopic vision, Sampati saw Sita in Lanka and gave the monkeys some valuable information.

"Sita is sitting under a tree in Ashok Vatika." Sampati revealed. "She's surrounded by many she-demons."

Sampati urged, "Sita must be rescued at once. You must cross the sea and rescue her at once."

Thanks to Sampati's help, the monkeys were hopeful again.

"Now, we know where Sita Mata is. We have to reach Lanka and get her back to Lord Rama," Hanuman addressed his troops.

But the monkeys were faced with a challenge when they tried to cross the ocean.

"Look at the vast stretch of ocean that lies between us and Lanka," the monkeys exclaimed. "How shall we cross the ocean and get to Lanka? It's impossible!"

"Lanka is a hundred yojanas (eight hundred miles) away," Jambavan informed the monkeys. "One of us must jump across the ocean to reach Lanka. Unfortunately, I'm old now and cannot jump so far."

Angad doubted his powers too. "I can reach Lanka, but I doubt if I'll have the strength to return," he confessed.

80 Jambavan Inspires Hanuman

Jambavan thought, *Only Hanuman is capable of crossing the ocean among all of us. But he does not realise his own prowess. I must remind him of his powers.* He then turned to Hanuman, who was silent.

"O great Hanuman," Jambavan said. "Why are you sitting silently? You are the son of the wind, and the epitome of wisdom and science. Only you can cross the ocean among all of us. Are you unaware of your own powers?"

When Hanuman was still silent, Jambavan said, "Remember, when you were just a child, you jumped up to seize the rising Sun thinking it to be a ripe fruit?"

Hanuman recalled the supernatural powers he had been blessed with by the gods.

"Nothing is impossible for you to achieve," Jambavan continued. "You have been incarnated on Earth to serve Lord Rama. Rise and jump across this mighty ocean! No one can surpass you in strength and speed!"

"Yes Jambavan, I shall fly to Lanka," Hanuman replied and assumed the gigantic form of a mountain.

"Glory to Hanuman!" the monkeys cheered.

81 Hanuman's Mighty Leap

After Jambavan reminded Hanuman of his supernatural capabilities, Hanuman was reminded of his powers to fly, become huge or small, become invisible, and all other extraordinary powers. Assuming the size of a huge mountain, Hanuman declared, "I shall destroy the city of Lanka and return with Sita Mata!"

"Now don't get carried away, Hanuman," Jambavan said. "All you have to do is find Sita and return here. That is the job assigned to us. The job of killing Ravana is Lord Rama's and not yours."

Motivated by Jambavan's talk, Hanuman nodded and turned to the group of monkeys.

"My brothers," he declared. "With the help of special powers bestowed upon me by Lord Rama, I am confident of crossing this ocean in a single leap."

"Jai Shri Ram," the overjoyed monkeys shouted. "Victory to Hanuman!"

Hanuman then prayed to Lord Rama. Then, he stood before the ocean and jumped high in the air. The monkeys watched in wonder as Hanuman sailed above the ocean at great speed.

"May you be victorious in your mission, O great Hanuman," Jambavan exclaimed happily.

82 Mount Mainak and Hanuman

A long time ago, mountains had the power to fly from one place to another. But the flying of these mountains and their landing caused the deaths of many humans and animals.

"From now onwards, mountains shall not fly but stay rooted in one place," Indra declared and cut off the wings of the mountains. The mountain named Mainak decided to hide in the ocean so that Indra couldn't cut off his wings.

When Hanuman took his flying leap over the ocean, the ocean advised Mount Mainak to emerge from the waters.

"Hanuman is going on Lord Rama's work," the ocean said to Mainak. "Since it's a long journey, let him rest on you."

As Hanuman flew across the ocean, a mountain rose suddenly and obstructed his path. Hanuman struck a blow at the mountain and it assumed the form of a human face.

"O Hanuman, I am Mount Mainak," the mountain said. "Please rest here for a while as it's a long journey ahead to Lanka."

"Thank you," Hanuman replied. "But I cannot rest till my mission is accomplished."

83 Hanuman Tricks Sursa

The demi-gods, sages and the gandharvas requested Sursa, the mother of the serpents to test Hanuman. *I shall take the form of a terrible snake demoness,* Sursa decided.

As Hanuman zoomed over the sea, Sursa obstructed his path in the terrible form of a sea monster. "The gods must have sent you to satisfy my hunger. Step into my mouth now!" Sursa said to Hanuman.

"I don't have the time now," Hanuman replied politely. "I'm going for an important mission. After it's done, I shall return and then you can eat me." Sursa was furious.

"No one can pass me without entering my mouth. Once you enter my mouth, you cannot get out alive. Prepare to die!"

"But can your mouth hold me?" Hanuman asked as Sursa widened her jaws to swallow Hanuman. Hanuman also kept increasing his size and soon Sursa's mouth resembled a huge giant. Hanuman suddenly became as small as a bee and entered Sursa's mouth. Then, he exited quickly before Sursa realised what was happening.

An impressed Sursa blessed Hanuman, "May you be successful in your mission!"

84 Hanuman Kills Simhika

A demoness named Simhika who lived in the ocean spotted Hanuman's shadow on the water as he flew overhead.

Now, I can have a good meal, Simhika thought. Using her magical powers, Simhika seized Hanuman's shadow on the water and dragged him down towards her.

Hanuman looked below to see the monstrous form of Simhika pulling at his shadow.

That demoness has trapped my shadow, Hanuman thought. *Sugreev had warned me about this demoness who can catch any flying creature just by holding its shadow in the water.*

Hanuman was drawn towards the demoness's mouth by a mysterious force. Simhika opened her jaws wide to swallow him. Hanuman grew to a monstrous size but Simhika opened her jaws wider. Hanuman quickly reduced his size and entered her mouth. Simhika thought she had gobbled up Hanuman, but was in for a rude shock. Hanuman expanded his size again after entering Simhika's stomach so that her body tore open and Simhika fell dead in the ocean. As the sharks rushed to feed on her dead body, Hanuman resumed his journey towards Lanka.

85 Hanuman Meets Lankini

Hanuman finally reached Lanka and landed on top of a hill. Taking an aerial view of the city, Hanuman was mesmerised by its sheer beauty.

What a pity that such a beautiful city will have to be destroyed, he thought. Hanuman decided to wait till sunset as a force of demons guarded Lanka. After sunset, he silently crept towards the city gates.

"Stop!" a voice commanded him. It was the none other than Lankini, the guardian deity of the city of Lanka. Lankini was a guard at Lord Brahma's abode who had been cursed to guard Lanka. Lankini shouted. "How dare you try and enter the city of Lanka when I'm there to protect it?"

Lankini was a fearsome demoness. She held a dangerous weapon in her hand. Just the sight of Lankini scared mighty warriors. But Hanuman only smiled at her.

"Where are you going?" Lankini exclaimed as Hanuman rushed past her. "No one can enter the city gates without my permission. Stop before I kill you!"

When Hanuman ignored Lankini, she attacked him.

86 Lankini Defeated

The guardian deity named Lankini attacked Hanuman when he tried to enter the city of Lanka.

I cannot attract undue attention to myself by fighting this creature and jeopardising my mission, Hanuman thought.

"I've arrived here just as a tourist to see the sights of Lanka," Hanuman assured Lankini. "Please allow me to enter."

This enraged Lankini further and she hit Hanuman.

Hanuman struck Lankini a hefty blow that sent her sprawling to the ground. *There, that'll take care of her for the moment*, Hanuman thought as he sped away inside Lanka.

Despite being felled and hurt by Hanuman, Lankini was happy because she remembered Lord Brahma's curse, "You shall be relieved of your curse to guard Lanka and return to Brahmalok after you are overcome by a monkey at Lanka's entrance."

"The days of Ravana are numbered. It has been foretold that the rakshashas shall cease to be invincible and Ravana's downfall will begin when I'm beaten by a monkey at the gates of Lanka. I fear that day has arrived," she mumbled to herself.

87 Hanuman Sees Mandodari

Hanuman entered Lanka. Using his divine powers, he had made himself very small so that no one would notice him. He started looking for Ashok Vatika where Sampati had said Sita Mata was kept.

Hanuman decided to enter Ravana's palace first. He wandered about and stopped at a bedroom where he saw a beautiful woman sleeping peacefully on a royal bed.

That must be Sita Mata, Hanuman thought. But then, a doubt arose in his mind. *How can Sita Mata be sleeping so peacefully in Ravana's palace after being separated from Lord Rama?* Hanuman wondered. *No, this is not Sita Mata. She must be one of Ravana's queens.* Hanuman was right in his guess. He had come across Ravana's queen Mandodari and mistakenly thought that she was Sita.

88 Hanuman Meets Vibheeshan

Hanuman left Ravana's palace, convinced that Sita wasn't there. He was also feeling rather hungry now. As he passed by another palace, he heard Lord Rama's name being chanted repeatedly.

Who has the courage to chant Lord Rama's name in Ravana's kingdom? Hanuman thought. He peeped inside. He saw a demon couple praying to Lord Rama. The person was Ravana's younger brother Vibheeshan, a staunch devotee of Lord Rama. Hanuman thought, *He is a devotee of Lord Rama, he will help me.* He entered the palace and bowed before Vibheeshan and his wife. "Jai Shri Ram," Hanuman exclaimed. "Who are you?" Vibheeshan asked Hanuman. "I'm a devotee of Lord Rama," Hanuman replied. "I'm also very hungry."

89 Vibheeshan Promises to Help Hanuman

Vibheeshan and his wife welcomed their guest and served him food and refreshments. Hanuman told them the actual purpose of his visit to Lanka. Vibheeshan told Hanuman that he had condemned Ravana after he kidnapped Sita, and advised him to return her to Lord Rama, but Ravana had paid no heed.

"Sita Mata is at Ashok Vatika," Hanuman said. "Can you help me locate Ashok Vatika as I must pass on Lord Rama's message to Sita?"

"I will help you in every way," Vibheeshan promised. He directed Hanuman to Ashok Vatika. "But be careful," he warned. "Ashok Vatika is heavily guarded by ferocious female demons as Ravana is hell bent on marrying Sita. But Sita, being a symbol of purity doesn't let Ravana come close to her."

90 Hanuman in Ashok Vatika

Hanuman was worried when he learned that Ravana was planning to marry Sita. "I must rescue Sita Mata," he exclaimed in anger. Vibheeshan told Hanuman that Ravana was cursed to die if he forcibly married a woman. So, he would not dare to marry Sita without her consent. Hanuman was very happy to have made a friend like Vibheeshan. Following Vibheeshan's directions, he easily located Ashok Vatika. He climbed the tallest tree in the grove and hid himself there so that no one could see him. Hanuman wandered through Ashok Vatika hopping from tree to tree.

Will I finally find Sita Mata in this huge grove? Hanuman thought to himself.

91 Hanuman Finds Sita

Hanuman wandered about the grove throughout the night in search of Sita. Finally, at daybreak, he spotted a beautiful woman sitting under a tree, guarded by ferocious she-demons.

There she is! I think I have found Sita Mata. Hanuman thought. Hanuman heard the she-demons threatening Sita.

"If you wish to live, agree to our Lord Ravana's request and marry him," they said. "Never!" Sita replied. "I shall die before that!"

Then, Hanuman heard a sudden commotion in the grove.

"Long live King Ravana," voices shouted as Ravana himself entered the grove in a procession.

Hanuman resisted the impulse to jump down and kill Ravana as he remembered Jambavan's advice about completing his mission.

Let me wait and watch what happens, he thought. Hanuman saw Ravana approach Sita under a tree as the she-demons respectfully moved away.

"Why do you wait for a husband who is not my match in strength, fame, valour or wealth?" Ravana demanded of Sita. "You have no choice. Sooner or later, you have to agree to be my queen. Be sensible and marry me now!"

92 Ravana Threatens Sita

Hanuman was sitting on the tree listening to Ravana asking Sita to marry her. *What nerve the scoundrel has*! Hanuman thought angrily. But Sita's reply really pleased him and he had to stop himself with great effort from joyously shouting 'Jai Shri Ram'. Sita placed a straw between Ravana and herself, enraging Ravana who knew that he would die if he crossed the straw because of the curse on him.

"Just as the sun cannot be separated from sunlight, you cannot separate my Lord Rama from me," Sita said proudly. "So give up your foolishness about wanting to marry me. If you wish to save your life, return me to My Lord and seek his protection before he kills you."

"I have had enough of your arrogance," a furious Ravana thundered. "I shall kill both your husband and you if you refuse to marry me."

After Ravana left, the she-demons approached Sita angrily. "How dare you refuse our lord again and again?" one of them demanded.

"Why don't you make our lord happy?" the second she-demon urged Sita. "Marry him!" They even threatened to kill Sita if she did not agree to marry Ravana.

93 Hanuman Intervenes

Sita felt so humiliated by Ravana and the she-demons that she decided to end her life. When Hanuman saw the grief-stricken Sita, he was afraid to approach her.

She is not herself, Hanuman thought. *If I approach her, she will get scared and think that it is Ravana in disguise. I must wait for her to calm down first.*

Sita untied the cord that held her hair together.

I shall end my life with this cord, she thought. Hanuman quickly reached the tree under which Sita was sitting and began to speak softly about the exploits of Rama.

"Rama, the great crown prince of Ayodhya, left for the forest accompanied by his wife Sita and his brother Lakshmana…" Hanuman began mumbling to himself.

Who can it be talking about my lord in this land of rakshasas? Sita thought.

"The wicked demon Ravana carried Sita away," Hanuman continued. "Thousands of monkeys were deputed by Lord Rama to find Sita but he had the most faith in Hanuman. I, Hanuman have finally found Sita Mata!"

"Oh, it's only a monkey," Sita looked up and exclaimed.

94 Rama's Ring

When Sita saw Hanuman sitting on the tree and chanting Lord Rama's name, she initially thought it was an illusion.

I am only seeing and hearing things that are related to My Lord, Sita thought. But Hanuman continued speaking about Lord Rama and jumped down the tree.

"Do not fear, Sita Mata," Hanuman reassured her. "I am Lord Rama's messenger, Hanuman. "Here is the ring he asked me to give you," Hanuman said, handing over Rama's ring to Sita. Sita was surprised to see the ring.

This is indeed my Lord Rama's signet ring. But how can he be here in Lanka? Sita thought.

"I am overcome with happiness to see My Lord's ring," she said to Hanuman, and was full of questions. "Where is he? Is he very worried about me? When will he rescue me? When will he kill this evil creature who wishes to defile me?"

"Lord Rama will rescue you very soon," Hanuman assured Sita. "No one but you occupies his mind. He does not know where you are, so he has sent me to find out."

95 Sita's Message

Hanuman assured Sita that she would soon be freed from Ravana's clutches. "I shall head back to Lord Rama and inform him that you are here," he said. "Lord Rama will immediately come with his army to rescue you from this evil Ravana. If you wish, I can carry you on my back to Lord Rama."

"No, Hanuman," Sita replied. "My honour will only be restored after Lord Rama comes to Lanka and destroys Ravana to take me with him. Please pass this message to him."

Hanuman bowed respectfully. Sita withdrew a jewel that she had kept concealed in her clothes and handed it over to Hanuman.

"Give this to My Lord," she said.

"I promise you that Lord Rama will be here soon. Ravana will fall by his arrow and you will be reunited with your Lord," Hanuman said. "Allow me to leave as I must reach Lord Rama with this news. But give me permission to eat some fruits from the grove first as I'm very hungry."

Sita smiled despite her sadness. "Please do so, Hanuman!" she said.

96 The Wicked Crow

Sita shared an incident with Hanuman before he left. "Once, Lord Rama and I were resting in a grove," Sita said. "Lord Rama fell asleep on my lap. Soon, a crow arrived and pecked me. I didn't know that it was Indra's son in disguise and threw a pebble to scare it away. But the crow continued pecking me. When Lord Rama awoke, he was very angry. He picked up a blade of grass and it turned into a powerful dart. Lord Rama threw it at the crow which flew away fearfully. But the dart continued chasing the crow even as it sought protection from Indra.

"'Only Lord Rama can protect you now,' Indra ordered. The crow flew back and fell at Lord Rama's feet to beg for forgiveness. The Lord asked the crow to apologise to me and I immediately forgave him. Remind Lord Rama of the incident."

Hanuman understood Sita's appeal for a speedy rescue. *The Lord had not spared a crow that had disturbed Sita. Surely Ravana deserves to be destroyed immediately for abducting her*, Hanuman thought.

97 Hanuman Destroys Ashok Vatika

Hanuman took leave of Sita and left. *Before leaving Lanka, let me satisfy my hunger and also fathom the strength of the enemy*, Hanuman thought.

He started eating the fruits in Ashok Vatika to satisfy his hunger. He began uprooting the trees there to attract the attention of the demons. The commotion alerted the armed guards in the garden. "Capture that impudent monkey before he destroys the beautiful grove," they cried. But as they rushed to capture Hanuman, he threw a tree at them that injured the guards who rushed to Ravana's palace to complain about the powerful monkey. *How can a single monkey cause so much trouble*? Ravana thought. *Indra must have sent a god disguised as a monkey.*

98 Hanuman Kills Akshaykumar

When the guards failed to catch Hanuman, Ravana ordered his youngest son Akshaykumar to catch him. Akshaykumar rode on his golden chariot that was drawn by eight horses. He found Hanuman sitting on a tree eating a mango. He screamed, "You monkey, surrender to me if you wish your life to be spared!"

Hanuman replied, "I only follow Lord Rama's orders." A furious Akshaykumar shot his deadly arrows at Hanuman, who caught and broke them. Then, Hanuman smashed Akshaykumar's golden chariot to pieces and killed him after a fierce battle.

99 Hanuman Destroys Meghnad's Army

Ravana was shocked when he heard that the destructive monkey had killed his son Akshaykumar. *If Indra has dared to send a warrior, I shall teach him a lesson. I shall send Indrajit himself,* he decided.

Ravana summoned his valiant son Meghnad who was also called Indrajit because he had defeated Lord Indra in battle. "Capture the monkey and bring him to me," Ravana ordered. Hanuman easily defeated the best warriors of Meghnad.He uprooted trees and threw them, injuring and killing the warriors. Meghnad was shocked to see his trained army defeated. "Why are you destroying this beautiful garden? What do you want?" he asked.

Hanuman munched on a fruit and didn't reply.

100 Meghnad Captures Hanuman

Meghnad was furious when Hanuman did not answer him. He shot an arrow at him, but was surprised when none of his powerful arrows hurt Hanuman.

Meghnad then decided to use his Brahmastra, the divine weapon given to him by Lord Brahma. He did not know that Hanuman had been blessed by Lord Brahma that the Brahmastra would not harm him. But Hanuman surrendered to the Brahmastra as a mark of respect to Lord Brahma. Besides, he also wished to meet Ravana and assess his strength before leaving Lanka. He fell down after the weapon struck him. Megnad immediately released his snake arrows to bind Hanuman. Hanuman was then dragged to Ravana's court by Meghnad's soldiers who laughed at him and mocked him. Hanuman remained silent.

101 Hanuman at Ravana's Court

Ravana was seated on his royal golden throne when Hanuman was led into his court."This is the monkey who has damaged Ashok Vatika," the soldiers informed Ravana.

"Who are you?" Ravana asked Hanuman. "My name is Hanuman, and I serve King Sugreev who is the king of the monkeys now. Vali is dead! He has been killed by Lord Rama."

"You shall be punished for killing my people and destroying my grove," Ravan shouted in rage.

"O vain king!" Hanuman replied. "No one can harm me as long as I am protected by Lord Rama. I allowed myself to be captured only to see you. I come to you as a messenger of Lord Rama."

102 Hanuman's Punishment

Ravana was furious after listening to Hanuman. He asked mockingly, "What is your message?"

"If you don't wish to die, release Sita Mata at once and beg Lord Rama's pardon," Hanuman replied. Ravana angrily ordered his soldiers to kill Hanuman at once. But his virtuous brother Vibheeshan stopped him. "An envoy cannot be put to death according to royal custom." Ravan knew that Vibheeshan was right. A king cannot put a royal messenger to death. But Hanuman had challenged him and also killed his son Akshaykumar. Ravana wished to teach Hanuman a lesson and also send across the message that whoever opposes him, is destroyed.

"I shall spare his life. But he shall be punished because of his offence. Tie a piece of cloth soaked in oil around his tail and set it on fire," Ravana ordered his soldiers.

103 Hanuman Breaks Free

Ravana's soldiers tied pieces of oil-soaked cloth around Hanuman's tail as Hanuman smiled. Hanuman kept elongating his tail and the soldiers soon ran out of cloth. "Set his tail on fire and walk him around the city to show everyone what happens to those who defy me," Ravana laughed loudly. With his tail set on fire, Hanuman was paraded through the streets of Lanka. Everyone laughed at the sight. As soon as the procession reached the city gates, Hanuman assumed a small form and freed himself of the ropes that bound him. As the ropes fell from his body, Hanuman assumed a gigantic form. "Look! the monkey has broken free!" the stunned soldiers exclaimed in helplessness and fear.

104 Hanuman Burns Down Lanka

When Lord Shiva decided to be incarnated on Earth as Hanuman to help Lord Rama kill Ravana, Parvati expressed the desire to be present in Hanuman's tail to burn down Lanka. Parvati was angry with Ravana because when he drove out his elder brother Kubera and became king of Lanka, he had occupied Parvati's palace which Kubera had gifted her. Hanuman set fire to the houses of Lanka with his burning tail. "Please spare our city, mighty one," Ravana's queen Mandodari pleaded.

"Ask your husband to repent for his sins, release Sita Mata and beg for Lord Rama's forgiveness," Hanuman roared angrily. Soon, most of Lanka was reduced to ashes. Among the few exceptions were Ashok Vatika and Vibheeshan's house.

105 The Creation of Lanka

Once, Lakshmi and Lord Vishnu paid a visit to Lord Shiva and Parvati in Mount Kailash where Lakshmi started shivering with cold. She asked Parvati, "You are a princess and used to the comforts of a palace. How can you stay in such a desolate and cold place like Mount Kailash?"

After some days, Lord Shiva and Parvati visited Vaikuntha. Parvati was amazed to see how beautiful Vaikuntha was. She pleaded with Lord Shiva to give her an equally beautiful palace. Lord Shiva summoned the divine architect Vishwakarma and the god of wealth Kubera."I want the finest palace in the world to be built for Parvati," Lord Shiva instructed them.

106 Parvati's Curse on Lanka

It was decided that Vishwakarma would do the engineering work while Kubera would provide the wealth needed to build a golden city right in the middle of the ocean. Parvati was thrilled to see the grand city and her palace. One day, while flying over the ocean, Ravana saw the beautiful city and wanted to possess it. He approached Lord Shiva disguised as a brahmin and as alms asked for Lanka.

"Lanka is yours, but you won't be able to live there for long since you have acquired it through false means," Lord Shiva told his greatest devotee Ravana. When Parvati came to know about Ravana's trick, she was enraged. "Lanka will be burnt down one day," Parvati cursed Ravana. This curse came true when Hanuman burnt down Lanka.

107 Dadhimukha Brings Good News

After reducing Lanka to ashes, Hanuman flew back to join his band of monkeys and Jambavan.Meanwhile, Rama was getting increasingly worried at Kishkindha when there was no positive news from the search parties.

"Your monkey armies have combed the entire regions of the north, east and west without any results," he said to Sugreev. "Will the search party that has gone south also return empty-handed?"

"I have great faith in the search party that has gone south," Sugreev replied. "That's because Ravana's kingdom Lanka lies to the south and that is why I have sent my strongest warriors, including Hanuman there."

"Look!" Lakshmana exclaimed, interrupting the conversation. "There's a monkey that is running towards us excitedly. It could be that he is a carrier of some good news." The monkey named Dadhimukha arrived and saluted Sugreev.

"My Lord, I am the protector of the garden named Madhuvana," he stated. "The garden has been completely ruined by Prince Angad, Hanuman and their followers. Every tree in the garden has been plundered of its fruits by the army of monkeys."

108 Hanuman Returns

Sugreev was elated when Dadhimukha arrived with the news that the monkeys were plundering Madhuvana Garden. "This is good news," Sugreev exclaimed. "This can only mean that they have found Sita. Hanuman and Angad must have allowed the monkeys to celebrate this joyous occasion by feasting on fruits and honey."

Rama and Lakshmana cast each other happy looks as Sugreev ordered Dadhimukha, "Let my victorious monkeys enjoy themselves as they have earned this reward. But tell Hanuman to come and see me immediately." After a while, Hanuman arrived and handed over Sita's jewel to Rama. "My Lord, I have found Sita Mata," Hanuman revealed. "Here is the jewel she asked me to give you." Rama took the jewel and stared at it in a trance. "Oh, Lakshmana," he said. "What could be more painful than beholding this jewel without Sita?"

"Hanuman, you have achieved the impossible," Rama said, embracing Hanuman.

109 Hanuman's Humility

Hanuman himself did not tell Rama about his heroics. Singing his own praises was contrary to his nature and he was happy that he had accomplished what he had set out to do. Jambavan told Rama about Hanuman's deeds.

"My Lord, a thousand narrations cannot do justice to what Hanuman has achieved during his journey to Lanka. But I shall try my best to tell you whatever had happened," Jambavan said to Rama. After listening to Hanuman's exploits from Jambavan, Rama was elated. He embraced Hanuman fondly.

"Hanuman, why did you not tell me about your adventures?" Rama said. "If Jambavan hadn't told me about them, I would have been deprived about your beautiful exploits."

"My Lord, finding a place in your heart is the greatest reward for a devotee like me," Hanuman said humbly after receiving Rama's embrace. "Recalling one's own exploits and receiving praise for it is not."

110 Rama's Army

At Rama's request, Hanuman described his adventures in Lanka and everyone was spellbound after listening to him."You have almost destroyed Lanka single-handedly, O brave Hanuman," Rama said admiringly.

When Hanuman was alone with Rama, he described the situation in which Sita was placed."My Lord, Sita Mata would not allow me to carry her away to you," Hanuman revealed. "She said that her honour would be restored only after you came to Lanka and vanquished Ravana." Rama thoughtfully agreed to leave for Lanka at once and rescue Sita.

"I shall consult with Sugreev and prepare the armies at once," Hanuman told Rama. Soon, Rama, Lakshmana, Sugreev, Hanuman, Angad and Jambavan assembled for a meeting to discuss their plans for invading Lanka. As Rama and Lakshmana did not have an army of their own, they relied on the powerful armies of the monkeys and the bears. A huge army was formed comprising monkeys and bears. Angad was named the commander of the monkey army while it was decided that Jambavan would lead the bears in battle.

111 Vibheeshan Meets Rama

Rama and Lakshmana, accompanied by Sugreev, Hanuman, Angad, Jambavan and the huge army of bears and monkeys set out for the long journey to Lanka. Finally, after a long march, they reached the southern tip of India, where the vast ocean stood in front of them and between them and Lanka. "My valiant soldiers," Rama declared. "We shall camp here till we find out a way to cross this great ocean and reach Lanka."

Meanwhile, at Ravana's court, his wife Mandodari and brother Vibheeshan both requested Ravana to set Sita free. But Ravana refused.When Vibheeshan insisted repeatedly, Ravana was angry with him and insulted him in front of everyone. *I must leave Lanka and join Lord Rama's forces.* Vibheeshan decided. *It's better to join the good forces rather than fight on the side of evil.* The monkeys were busy setting up camp by the ocean when they saw five rakshasas flying towards them."We are under attack by the demons," a monkey cried. "Be prepared to fight!" But the rakshasas were unarmed and Hanuman recognised Vibheeshan as their leader. "Stop!" he ordered the monkeys who were about to attack the demons. Hanuman respectfully led Vibheeshan to Sugreev and Rama.

112 Rama Welcomes Vibheeshan

Vibheeshan bowed respectfully after he was led to Rama and Sugreev. "I'm Ravana's younger brother Vibheeshan," he introduced himself. "I urged Ravana repeatedly to release Sita and restore her to Lord Rama but he always refused. This time, he insulted me before the entire court. Hence, I have arrived here with a few of my trusted aides to join Lord Rama." Sugreev urged Vibheeshan to rest for a while and then discussed the matter with Rama, Lakshmana and Hanuman. "I suspect a conspiracy," Sugreev said. "I don't think we should trust Ravana's brother. We should kill him." "No, Sugreev," Rama said. "Anyone who comes seeking refuge from me shall receive it."

"I have met Vibheeshan in Lanka," Hanuman stated. "He is the only one who helped me there. He can be trusted blindly. Vibheeshan will also be useful for us to gauge the military strength and tactics of Ravana's army." When Vibheeshan arrived, Rama embraced him and welcomed him to join his forces.

113 Sagara Appears

Hanuman was worried about how Lord Rama's huge army would cross the ocean and reach Lanka. *Maybe Vibheeshan will have a solution to the problem*, Hanuman thought and brought Vibheeshan to Rama. Vibheeshan advised Rama to pray to Sagara, the god of the ocean, to help them cross the ocean and reach Lanka.

Rama fasted for three days and prayed to Sagara.

"O god of the ocean," he prayed. "Please help me by creating a path across the ocean so that my army can reach Lanka and I can rescue Sita."

But when Sagara didn't respond after three days, Rama's anger was aroused. "O Sagara, you have mistaken my patience for my weakness," Rama thundered, and picked up his bow and arrows to aim at the ocean. "I shall dry up the waters of the ocean with my arrows so that my army can cross over to Lanka by foot."

Seeing that Rama would surely destroy him, Sagara rose immediately from the ocean. "Forgive me, My Lord," he said, bowing before Rama.

114 A Bridge Across the Ocean

When Rama threatened to destroy the ocean, Sagara rose up and bowed before Rama."O Rama, build a bridge over my waters to reach Lanka. I promise to hold up that bridge!" Sagara said. Rama consulted Sugreev and Hanuman. Hanuman suddenly remembered the monkey brothers Nal and Neel.

He said to Rama, "We can build a bridge easily with the help of Nal and Neel who are expert builders."

"But how can two monkeys build such a huge bridge?" Rama enquired doubtfully.

"All of us will build the bridge under their supervision," Hanuman stated.

"Nal and Neel were very naughty during childhood," Sugreev explained. "They used to torment a sage by throwing away his belongings into the water. Finally, the sage cursed the brothers that whatever they throw into the water will float instead of sinking."

"This curse will be helpful for us to build the bridge," Hanuman added. "We will carry the raw material to the brothers who will throw it into the water to create a floating bridge."

Rama smiled finally. "Let us begin," he declared.

115 Nala and Neela Help

Nala and Neela were summoned. Rama ordered them to begin the construction of the bridge over the ocean. Nala was given the task of supervising over the construction of the bridge.

"Go in several directions to fetch huge rocks, trees and boulders," Nala ordered. The monkeys assigned themselves in several small groups and set off. Soon, they returned carrying huge boulders, stones and trees.

Rama and Lakshmana were very happy with the dedication, hard work and sincerity of the monkeys. The monkeys formed a huge queue and passed the rocks and trees to the end of the queue where Nala and Neela stood. Nala and Neela threw the rocks and trees into the ocean where they floated. These were then fastened together to form the initial parts of the bridge on the ocean.

The bridge will take a long time to be built this way, Hanuman thought. "Jai Shri Ram!" Hanuman chanted and assumed a gigantic size. Then, he flew away to return with huge mountains and rocks. Everyone was surprised at this feat.

"Glory to Hanuman!" the monkeys shouted.

116 Hanuman's Devotion

Hanuman did not need Nala and Neela's help to make the huge boulders and stones float on the ocean. After collecting huge mountains, Hanuman just wrote Rama's name on each stone and threw them in the ocean so that they floated easily. Everyone marvelled at the sheer devotion of Hanuman. Even Rama was surprised that the stones Hanuman threw into the ocean floated on it.

"What are you writing on the stones, O Hanuman?" Rama asked.

"My Lord, I am writing your name on the stones. See, they are floating easily. Otherwise it will take a long time to build this bridge."

Hanuman's devotion is unmatched, Rama thought. *I must help him. If these stones and boulders are floating by just writing my name on it, they should also float when I throw them.*

But when Rama wrote his name on a huge boulder, picked it up and threw it in the ocean, it sank immediately.

Oh, something has gone wrong, a surprised Rama thought. He picked up another boulder and tried again, but that too sank.

117 Rama Fails

Rama thought that if he too wrote his name on the rocks and boulders just like Hanuman, they would also float on the ocean.

"What are you doing, My Lord?" Hanuman asked Rama. Rama was silent as he could not match Hanuman's devotion.

"My Lord, the stones that I'm writing on are floating only because of your association with the stone," Hanuman explained. "But when you are throwing the stone into the water, you are rejecting the stones or the offerings made in your name, unlike me, who is offering the stone in the worship of your name. Once you reject the stones, how can they float?"

"I was trying to help you build the bridge quickly, O great Hanuman," Rama replied. "But I realise now that no one in the world can match your unparalleled devotion. Not even I can do the tasks that you can. You will henceforth be known as the greatest devotee on Earth."

"Jai Shri Ram," Hanuman shouted, bowing to Lord Rama. The other monkeys echoed his shout as they built the bridge with renewed enthusiasm.

118 The Spider, the Squirrel and Rama

When Hanuman was hoisting huge mountain tops into the ocean, he noticed a small spider brushing small particles of dust into the water with its legs to assist the building of the bridge.

Hanuman was about to brush off the spider when he was stopped by Rama. "Let the spider work, Hanuman," Rama gently said. "The devotional service of the spider is as satisfying to me as yours."

Suddenly, the monkeys saw a squirrel throwing small pebbles into the water and started laughing. "No one's effort goes in vain if it is done with the right kind of spirit and devotion," Rama addressed the monkeys."You might think that the spider and the squirrel's contribution is insignificant. But the dust thrown by the spider and the pebbles thrown by the squirrel will actually join the bigger rocks together."

119 Ravana's Daughter

According to the Thai and Cambodian 'Ramayana', Ravana also had a daughter. This princess was a beautiful mermaid who was named Suvarnamacha or 'the golden mermaid' because her body glistened like gold.

When Rama's monkey army was building the bridge, Ravana summoned his daughter Suvarnamacha. "Go with your people and prevent the bridge from being built," Ravana ordered. Suvarnamacha and her mermaid army immediately swam underwater to reach the place where the monkeys were building the bridge. The monkeys were surprised when they saw that the stones that they flung into the ocean disappeared after floating for a while.

"The rocks are sinking," a monkey exclaimed.

That's impossible! Hanuman thought. *According to the curse of the sage on Nala and Neela, anything they throw in water must float. The monkey army is using this curse to their advantage. How can it go wrong*?

120 Hanuman Meets Suvarnamacha

When Hanuman saw the rocks thrown by the monkeys into the water disappearing, he became suspicious and decided to investigate. Asking the monkeys to rest for a while, Hanuman dived under the ocean. He spotted the mermaids underwater stealing the rocks and dragging them under the ocean.

Hanuman followed them who unknowingly led them to their leader Suvarnamacha.

"Who are you?" Hanuman challenged the princess after introducing himself. "Why are you trying to stop us from building the bridge?"

Suvarnamacha was afraid as Hanuman could single-handedly wipe out her entire tribe.

"I am following the orders of my father, Ravana," she informed Hanuman.

"You must stop disturbing our work immediately or I shall be forced to take strong action. Tell Ravana that he could not stop us from building the bridge because of me. He has invited this upon himself by abducting Lord Rama's wife, Sita Mata. As a woman how can you support such an act even if it has been done by your own father?" Hanuman asked.

Suvarnamacha was ashamed and returned the stones which she and her mermaids had stolen.

121 Shani and Hanuman

It is believed that the planet Saturn or Shani visits each person once in their lifetime for a period of seven and a half years. This is also known as saade-saati. Shani descended on Hanuman when he was busy building the bridge over the ocean.

"Please postpone your visit to a later date," Hanuman requested Shanidev.

"Why?" Shani demanded.

"Wait till I successfully complete Lord Rama's task," Hanuman requested Shani humbly with folded hands. "Let me finish building this bridge and help Lord Rama defeat Ravana's army to regain Sita Mata."

But the arrogant Shani refused to wait for so long.

"No!" he said adamantly. "I must descend on you right now!" Hanuman realised that he had no option but to bow down to Shani's demand.

"Please sit on my head," Hanuman requested Shani. "My hands are busy building this bridge and my legs are too lowly for you to sit on."

Shani happily descended on Hanuman's head and sat there while Hanuman continued with his work calmly as if nothing had happened.

122 Hanuman Teaches Shani a Lesson

Shani settled on Hanuman's head, dismissing Hanuman's request to wait till he had finished his work of finishing the bridge and helping Rama defeat Ravana. Hanuman continued with his work. He piled heavy boulders and stones on his head on which Shani was sitting, and carried them. As the weight of the piles of stones and boulders on Hanuman's head began increasing and were replaced by huge mountains, Shani found it impossible to sit on Hanuman's head with so much weight on it.

I'm getting suffocated, Shani thought. *I must escape before this weight crushes me*!

"Carry on with your work. I must leave now!" Shani said respectfully.

"But you must sit on my head for seven and a half years. You cannot leave now!" Hanuman insisted.

"Please allow me to leave, Hanuman," Shani pleaded. "It's already seven and a half minutes since I sat on your head and it feels like seven and a half years."

Hanuman allowed Shani to leave and since then, the devotees of Hanuman have discovered that the ill-effects of Shani are considerably lessened if they worship Hanuman devotedly.

123 Hanuman and Mount Govardhan

Hanuman decided to fly and fetch a huge mountain from the Himalayas. However, he got delayed. While he was crossing Vrindavan, a messenger from Sugreev informed him that the bridge to Lanka was almost ready now. "King Sugreev has sent a message that no further materials will be needed for the bridge," the messenger relayed to Hanuman.

What shall I do with this huge mountain? Hanuman thought. *If I carry it back to the Himalayas, it will be too late for me to join the troops marching to Lanka. I have to leave the mountain here.* The mountain named Govardhan was disappointed that it did not get an opportunity to serve Lord Rama. "You got me from the Himalayas promising that I shall be employed in the service of Lord Rama," Mount Govardhan complained. "But now as you have no use for me, you are abandoning me here in the middle of nowhere." "Don't worry," Hanuman assured the mountain. "You shall get an opportunity to serve Lord Rama in his next incarnation as Krishna."

124 Hanuman and Shiva

While the monkeys were making the bridge, Rama decided to worship Lord Shiva and seek his blessings to win the war. He instructed Hanuman to go to Kashi immediately where Lord Shiva was at the time, and get the Shivalinga from him before the time allotted for the worship.

Hanuman flew to Kashi. Lord Shiva handed him the Linga and praised him, "If you were not there, this Dham would not have been built. Who else could have reached here so quickly?" Lord Shiva's genuine praise went to Hanuman's head and he became proud of his achievement.

125 The Sand Lingam

After receiving Lord Shiva's praise, there was false pride in Hanuman now, instead of devotion. As he flew back from Kashi to Rama with the lingam from Lord Shiva, he became very relaxed because of his arrogance. The thought of reaching before the muhurt as per Rama's orders did cross Hanuman's mind once, but he dismissed the thought.

I shall reach before the allotted time is over for the worship, Hanuman thought confidently. *Otherwise, I shall stop the muhurt.*

Meanwhile, Rama was getting worried as the auspicious time for the worship of Lord Shiva was about to end. He asked the assembled sages for advice.

"It is the worship that is more important than the means," the sages advised Rama. "Make a lingam out of the wet sand and worship Lord Shiva."

Rama did as advised by the sages and soon the lingam was ready.

When Hanuman arrived and saw that Rama had already created the lingam, he was upset with Rama for having sent him all the way to Kashi to get the lingam from Lord Shiva.

126 Hanuman's Pride Broken

Hanuman was upset with Rama for making him fly all the way to Kashi. He felt that his efforts were wasted. He expressed his thoughts to Rama.

"I did so because the auspicious time for the worship was about to end, Hanuman," Rama explained. "Why don't you replace the sand lingam with the lingam you have brought?"

It never crossed Hanuman's mind that it wouldn't be right to break the sand lingam. His pride dominated as he pulled at the sand lingam. But to Hanuman's surprise, the lingam did not move an inch. Instead, Hanuman received a shock and fell unconsciousness. Rama quickly revived Hanuman.

"Are you all right, Hanuman?" he asked worriedly. Hanuman got up and fell at Rama's feet to beg for his pardon.

"I was a fool to question your actions, My Lord," Hanuman said as he understood everything. "Please forgive me. How can the lingam formed by your hands ever break when the rocks and boulders on which your name is written float on the very ocean?"

127 Rama Worships Lord Shiva

Rama embraced Hanuman lovingly after the latter asked for his forgiveness. Then Rama worshipped the sand lingam that he had created and prayed to Lord Shiva. Pleased by his devotion, Shiva appeared before Rama and blessed him. At Rama's request, Lord Shiva established himself in the lingam.

Thus, the famous 'Rameshwar Jyotirling' came into being and is worshipped till date. The place in South India where Rama had worshipped the sand lingam became known as Rameshwaram. Later, Rama also worshipped Devi Durga, to bless him before his battle with Ravana.

Soon, the bridge was complete. Then, the huge army of bears and monkeys led by Rama and Lakshmana marched towards Lanka on that bridge. As promised to Rama, Sagara, the lord of the ocean ensured that the bridge held when the mighty monkeys and bears walked over it.

128 Ravana Creates an Illusion

Meanwhile, Ravana's spies had brought him the news that Vibheeshan had joined forces with Rama's army which was now crossing the sea and approaching Lanka.Then Ravana created a false head of Rama and went to Sita. Throwing the head before her, he said, "My soldiers have killed your husband Rama. Here is his head!"

"Oh, My Lord Rama!" Sita hugged the head and cried. Ravana threatened to kill her as well if she did not marry him.

A kind demoness named Sarama revealed the truth to Sita, "Ravana has created an illusion to trick you into thinking that your husband is dead. In fact, Lord Rama is now on his way to Lanka with a huge army to rescue you."

129 Ravana Prepares for War

Rama and his army crossed the ocean and set up camp on the outskirts of Lanka on Mount Suvela. Ravana's ministers advised him to return Sita to Rama and befriend him. Ravana exclaimed angrily, "How can a mortal like Rama be my equal, who, with only an army of monkeys, dares to challenge my might?"

"Remember what one monkey did to Lanka," a minister warned him. "The monkeys are no match for the Asuras. Rama might have crossed the ocean to reach Lanka but he shall not return alive. Prepare for war!" Ravana decided to assess the strength of Rama's army and climbed to the top of the ramparts. From there, he had a clear look at Rama's army.

130 Rama's Peace Mission

Sugreev had long wanted to prove his prowess to Rama. He leaped and landed where Ravana was standing at the ramparts of his palace. Sugreev flung away Ravana's diadem that adorned his ten heads. A furious Ravana attacked Sugreev who was forced to flee for his life.

Rama then decided to send Prince Angad as messenger to Ravana's court as an effort to avoid war.

"It is not too late to save yourself, O Ravana," Angad threatened Ravana in his court. "If you return Sita to Lord Rama and apologise, he will surely spare your life and this war can be avoided."

"Seize that impudent monkey and kill him," Ravana ordered angrily. But Angad escaped easily.

131 The War Begins

When Angad informed Rama about the failure of the peace mission, the army prepared to invade Lanka. The demons were equipped with deadly weapons and magical powers. Rama's army chanted Lord Rama's name to gain strength to fight them. Then Hanuman emitted a thunderous cry and increased his size to attack. Utterly scared, the demons began to flee. But the monkeys caught them and started throwing them into the ocean, or leaped up to the battlements and dragged the defending rakshasas down.

The monkeys had the upper hand in the battle during the day but as evening neared, the demons got stronger because of their magical powers. But Hanuman and Angad terrorised the demons and Rama and Lakshmana felled them with their arrows.

132 Garuda Saves Lakshmana

Ravana's son Indrajit made himself invisible and showered arrows of poisonous snakes on Rama and Lakshmana, who fell unconscious. Rama soon regained consciousness and placing Lakshmana's head on his lap he tried to revive him. Suddenly, Garuda, the divine eagle and the enemy of snakes flew to the battlefield and landed beside Rama. He caressed Lakshmana with his wings who regained consciousness at once.

Hanuman was enraged that Indrajit had used treacherous means. With a huge roar, he unleashed himself upon the rakshasas. Many of Ravana's powerful generals like Dhumraksha and Prahasta were killed by Hanuman.

133 Lakshmana Injured Again

Indrajit attacked the monkey army again using his deadly arrows. Enraged, Hanuman uprooted a mountain and threw it at Indrajit. Indrajit rose into the air with his magical powers and attacked Hanuman from the skies. Now, Lakshmana came to Hanuman's aid and was locked in a fierce battle with him.

Indrajit invoked the Shakti, his deadliest weapon given to him by Lord Brahma and released it at Lakshmana. The arrow hit Lakshmana on the chest and he fell down unconscious. Hanuman was shocked at the sight as the demons celebrated. "Lakshmana is dead!" the demons rejoiced.

But how can Lakshmana die? Hanuman thought. *It's impossible! He is Lord Rama's brother and always under his protection!*

134 Hanuman Fetches Sushen

Indrajit again wounded Lakshmana. Hanuman quickly carried the unconscious Lakshmana to the grief-stricken Rama.

"Only Sushen, the best physician available in Lanka can cure Lakshmana," Vibheeshan advised Rama. Rama ordered Hanuman to fetch Sushen at once. Hanuman lifted the whole of Sushen's house and flew back. On Vibheeshan and Rama's request, Sushen examined Lakshmana. "Only a herb named Sanjeevani can save Lakshmana's life," Sushen declared. "Where can this herb be found?" Rama asked anxiously.

"It's available only in the Himalayas and must be fetched before sunrise," Sushen replied.

135 Hanuman and Kalanemi

When the physician Sushen spoke about the magical herb that would cure Lakshmana, Rama requested Hanuman to bring it at once. Sushen reminded him to get it before sunrise.

Rama blessed Hanuman as he leaped high in the air. As Hanuman was on his way to get the life-saving herb, he was very hungry and thirsty. As he flew over a lake, he decided to drink water.

Ravana's spies had informed him of Hanuman's mission. Ravana had sent a demon named Kalanemi to spoil the same. Kalanemi knew that Hanuman would stop for a drink and had assumed the form of a holy sage, sitting by this lakc, waiting for Hanuman to arrive.

136 Hanuman and the Crocodile

As Hanuman landed to drink water, he spotted the sage sitting beside the lake, chanting Rama's name. He did not know that the sage was actually the demon Kalanemi in disguise. Hanuman paid his respects to the holy man before drinking water. The sage offered the cool water from his vessel for Hanuman to drink which was poisoned. Hanuman said that the water was not enough to quench his thirst.

"Drink the water from the lake then," Kalanemi said. As Hanuman entered the lake and started drinking water, a huge crocodile grabbed his foot and pulled him underwater. Hanuman shook his foot free and after a brief fight, killed the crocodile. He was about to exit the lake when he was surprised to see a divine being rise from the crocodile's dead body.

137 Hanuman Kills Kalanemi

The divine being that rose from the crocodile's dead body bowed before Hanuman and revealed that he had been relieved of a curse to remain a crocodile. He warned him that the sage sitting by the lake was a demon named Kalanemi sent by Ravana to kill him.

A furious Hanuman attacked the false sage. Kalanemi assumed his true form and a fierce fight began. Hanuman overpowered Kalanemi and killed him.

Hanuman then again flew towards the Himalayas. He soon arrived before the Drongiri Mountain where the magical herb known as the Sanjeevani would be found. But there were so many herbs there that Hanuman was totally confused as to which of them was Sanjeevani.

138 Hanuman Lifts the Mountain

Hanuman was confused when he saw so many herbs on the Drongiri Mountain. He couldn't make out which one was the Sanjeevani herb. Suddenly, an idea struck Hanuman.

Sushen could pick the right herb for himself. "Jai Shri Ram!" Hanuman chanted, and uprooted the huge Drongiri Mountain and flew with it towards Lanka. Hanuman was so strong that the massive mountain seemed like a bunch of flowers to him. On his return journey, Hanuman had to cross the city of Ayodhya. As he flew over Ayodhya, the shadow of Hanuman and the mountain fell on Ayodhya, alarming the people.

139 Bharat Meets Hanuman

The shadow of Hanuman and the mountain he was carrying fell on the city. The people of Ayodhya panicked that demons have attacked them. Rama's brother Bharat, who was ruling the kingdom on Rama's behalf released a powerful arrow from his bow which struck Hanuman. Bharat ran towards him and was surprised to see the huge monkey uttering Rama's name. Hanuman narrated the entire sequence of events to Bharat who repented having shot down a friend and apologised to Hanuman.

"Do not worry, my lord," Hanuman said. "Your arrow just stunned me. But I should be leaving as it will be sunrise soon."

140 Hanuman Leaves Ayodhya

Bharat was relieved and also surprised that his arrow had not injured Hanuman. He was also enraged to learn about Sita's abduction by Ravana and decided to march towards Lanka to help Rama. But Hanuman assured him that Rama would surely defeat Ravana and he would want Bharat to look after his Ayodhya. Bharat then respectfully bid farewell to Hanuman. He said he was confident that his dear brother Lakshmana's life would be saved with Hanuman in charge of that mission. Both embraced warmly.

"Jai Shri Ram!" Hanuman shouted and increased his form to a gigantic size to fly away from Ayodhya. Everyone watched, mesmerised.

141 Lakshmana Is Revived

Hanuman carried the mountain across the ocean to arrive in Lanka before sunrise. He told Sushen that he carried the whole mountain since he could not recognise the right herb. Sushen crushed the Sanjeevani herb and held it under Lakshmana's nose who regained consciousness. Rama thanked Sushen and hugged Hanuman, "You are as dear to me as Lakshmana," he said. The other injured monkeys also got cured with the mountain's purifying air.

"Please return the mountain to its original place, Hanuman," Rama requested and Hanuman flew away again.

142 Lord Shaligram's Idol

Hanuman returned the Drongiri Mountain to its proper place. While returning to Lanka he descended near the river Ghantaki to bathe where he found an idol of Lord Shaligram. He flew towards Lanka with the idol and reached the Kamal Teerth by evening, where he stopped to offer prayers. He could not pray holding the idol nor could it be placed on the ground. He looked for someone who would hold the idol for him, but there was no one.

143 Hanuman and the Mountain

Hanuman was unable to offer his evening prayers. Suddenly, he saw a divine woman. Hanuman requested her to hold the idol. The woman agreed but asked him to return soon. Hanuman began chanting Lord Rama's name and was so immersed in his worship that he totally lost track of time and forgot about the woman. When he opened his eyes, he saw a huge mountain standing before him.

How did this mountain appear here all of a sudden? Hanuman wondered. Then he saw the divine woman and requested her to return the idol of Lord Shaligram.

144 Hanuman and Goddess Mahalakshmi

Hanuman requested the woman to return the idol but she said that she had kept the idol on the ground and it had become a mountain. Hanuman wanted to take the mountain to Lanka, but could not lift it.

Then a voice said, "The divine woman is Goddess Mahalakshmi performing penance to be reunited with Lord Vishnu. After killing Hiranyakashipu in his Narasimha Avatar, Lord Vishnu took the form of a Shaligram. He wished to bless his devotees here so he chose you to carry him in the form of this idol. Henceforth this place will be known as Naamagiri Kshetra."

145 Hanuman Kills Ravana's Generals

After Sushen revived Lakshmana, the battle between Rama and Ravana's army intensified. Ravana sent a powerful demon named Dhumraksh to lead his army. Hanuman killed Dhumraksh with a fierce blow from his mace.

Mahodar was the next general but Hanuman attacked his army with uprooted trees and felled them with his mace.Mahodar challenged Hanuman to a duel. A furious Hanuman jumped upon Mahodar and after a brief fight, killed him. Then Ravana decided to enter the battlefield himself.

146 Rama Humiliates Ravana

Ravana caused panic among the army of monkeys. Rama climbed on to Hanuman's shoulders to fight Ravana. His arrows shattered Ravana's chariot and killed his charioteer and horses. His bow and diadem were also shattered by Rama's arrows. Ravana stood totally at Rama's mercy. Rama said, "As you are unarmed, I won't kill you now. Return to fight me tomorrow!"

An embarrassed Ravana silently returned to his palace to plot his revenge against Rama. He summoned his generals,"Rama must be defeated at any cost. Kumbhakarna is our only hope now. Wake him up immediately!" Ravana ordered urgently.

147 Kumbhakarna Woken Up

As Ravana's brother Kumbhakarna had become too powerful, the gods tricked him to remain in deep slumber for six months. Now as Ravana ordered to wake him up, the demons created a great din by beating drums, blowing conches and trumpets, but failed. Finally, a great feast was laid, the aroma of which entered his nostrils and woke up the sleeping giant. After learning that Rama had invaded Lanka, Kumbhakarna condemned Ravana for abducting someone else's wife. Then he said, "It's my duty to obey you. Tell me whom I have to fight."

"You must defeat Rama," Ravana replied. "But first, you must kill Hanuman."

148 Sugreev Captured

Kumbhakarna arrived in the battlefield with his huge size. After he defeated all the great monkey warriors, Hanuman arrived to fight him. A mighty battle began between the two warriors in which none could defeat the other. Then Kumbhakarna grabbed Sugreev and held him high. Hanuman thought of assuming a huge form and rescuing Sugreev.

But then he thought, *I cannot kill Kumbhakarna as he is destined to die at the hands of Lord Rama.* He decided to let Sugreev escape from Kumbhakarna himself.

149 Kumbhakarna's Secret

When Sugreev realised that he had been captured by Kumbhakarna, he bit his ear. Kumbhakarna loosened his grip on Sugreev, who immediately escaped. Kumbhakarna returned to the battlefield.

Vibheeshan immediately warned Rama to beware of Kumbhakarna who was the most dangerous demon. "He can be killed only after his powers have been weakened considerably. According to a boon received by Kumbhakarna, he can be weakened only by someone who hasn't slept for fourteen years and has had limited food for the same period of time."

150 Lakshmana to Fight Kumbhakarna

Hanuman said to Rama, "Your brave brother Lakshmana has not slept for fourteen years having kept constant watch over you all this while to ensure that you sleep peacefully. Lakshmana has also had very little food. Only he can weaken the invincible Kumbhakarna in battle." Rama thanked Hanuman for his wise counsel. "Go and fight Kumbhakarna, Lakshmana," Rama instructed. "After you have fought with him, I shall put an end to his life." Accompanied by Hanuman, Lakshmana went to meet Kumbhakarna in battle.

151 Kumbhakarna Warns Ravana

"Tomorrow you have to kill Rama in battle," Ravana said to Kumbhakarna even though he knew that he wouldn't be able to stay awake for long as he had been prematurely awakened from his sleep.

Although Kumbhakarna hadn't fought with Rama, he had seen him and was dazzled by the blue brilliance from Rama's body. He thought, *This is the man whom they say is Narayana himself. Why did Ravana make the mistake of abducting his wife*? A worried Kumbhakarna then warned Ravana, "I suspect that Rama is an incarnation of Lord Vishnu himself. Rama and Lakshmana are not ordinary mortals."

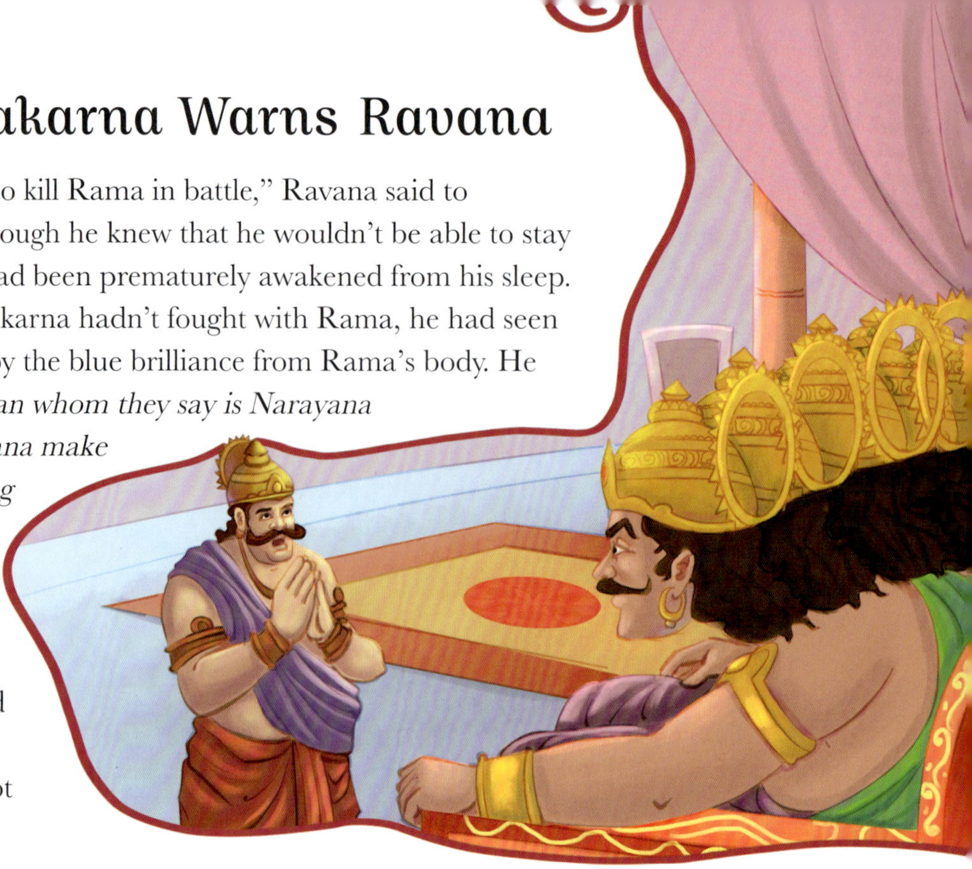

152 Kumbhakarna's Advice

Kumbhakarna advised Ravana to return Sita to Rama. This made Ravana angry and he mocked, "My own brother, who could not even kill the monkey Hanuman, is discouraging me."

Kumbhakarna thought, *Ravana has lost all sense of reasoning*. He replied, "I have realised that Hanuman is an incarnation of Lord Shiva. It was impossible for him to fight like that otherwise. I shall prove in the battlefield that I am not a coward. But one has to face the truth. Rama and Hanuman are both incarnations of Lord Vishnu and Shiva. As a younger brother, I cannot advise you further."

153 Hanuman Advises Lakshmana

Hanuman advised Lakshmana to only weaken Kumbhakarna, not kill him, which only Lord Rama was destined to do. Hanuman explained, "Overeating and oversleeping dulls the demon's brain. You have not slept and have eaten minimally. Hence, you are the lightness that will dispel the darkness of Kumbhakarna before Lord Rama kills him." "Lead me to Kumbhakarna, Hanuman," Lakshmana ordered. Hanuman took Lakshmana on his shoulders and flew towards Kumbhakarna.

154 Lakshmana Fights Kumbhakarna

Lakshmana stopped Kumbhakarna's progress and challenged him to a fight. Kumbhakarna did not wish to fight with anyone else. "Where is Rama?" he shouted. "To get to Rama, you must fight me first," Lakshmana retorted. "My fight is with Rama and not with you." Kumbhakarna replied. "Just like you are following your elder brother's orders, so am I," Lakshmana said.

A fierce fight began between the two warriors. *I must use sorcery to defeat him*, Kumbhakarna thought. A hundred Kumbhakarnas appeared to fight. Lakshmana was confused. Then, with the help of his divine weapons he destroyed all the false forms of Kumbhakarna.

155 Kumbhakarna Fights Rama

Lakshmana and Kumbhakarna fought for hours. Hanuman was worried as this duel was leading to a heavy loss of lives in the monkey army who were caught in the line of Kumbhakarna's fury. Hanuman advised Lakshmana to stop fighting as Kumbhakarna had been considerably weakened by now. Lakshmana let him approach Rama, and a deadly fight began between the two. Kumbhakarna released a weapon which started raining boulders. All of Kumbhakarna's divine weapons were successfully countered by Rama.

Not even Indra is capable of countering these weapons, Kumbhakarna thought. *Rama can be none other than Lord Vishnu*!

156 Kumbhakarna Dead

Following Vibheeshan's advice, Rama invoked a divine arrow which cut off Kumbhakarna's huge body part by part, finally piercing his heart and killing him. Sugreev ordered his soldiers to set fire to Lanka. The demons fled in fear. But the monkeys stopped as they saw Ravana's son Indrajit approaching on a chariot on which he held a woman hostage whom Hanuman recognised as Sita. As the monkeys charged towards Indrajit, he threatened to kill Sita there and then.

157 Indrajit's Illusory Powers

The monkeys stopped when Indrajit threatened to kill Sita with a raised sword. Saying that, "Sita is the cause of this war," Indrajit killed her with his sword in front of the stunned monkeys. He thought, *Now, I shall have some respite before the monkeys attack again. Before they return, I shall perform the Nikumbhil yajna to make me invincible in the battle.*

He raced away his chariot to perform the sacred yajna, and the monkeys raced to Rama to give him the news of Sita's death. Vibheeshan consoled the weeping Rama, "Sita is alive! Indrajit has created an illusory Sita using his magical powers."

158 Indrajit's Yajna Spoiled

Vibheeshan comforted Rama that Sita was alive. "Indrajit has distracted us to perform the Nikhumbil Yajna to make him invincible," he explained. Rama dispatched Lakshmana with a small troop of monkeys led by Hanuman to stop the yajna. As they entered the cave where he was meditating, Indrajit escaped with his magical powers swearing revenge on the battlefield.

Vibheeshan said, "Indrajit cannot be killed as long as he is fighting on his chariot, the Agniratha, which is a symbol of his power granted by his Kuldevi Nikumbala."

159 Indrajit Killed

Vibheeshan revealed to Lakshmana, "If you destroy Indrajit's Agniratha, the powers that protect him will be finished." Lakshmana's powerful arrow broke the wheels of Indrajit's chariot and killed his charioteer, forcing Indrajit to jump to the ground to prevent being killed. None of his weapons or sorcery were working, so he flew back towards Lanka and returned with a new chariot and charioteer. But this was a normal chariot. Lakshmana invoked a divine arrow and released it, killing Ravana's mighty son at once.

160 Ravana Meets Mahiravan

Ravana's courage broke as he had lost all his sons, generals and brothers in the battle. He decided to seek the help of his brother, Mahiravana and went to the netherworld to meet him."Rama and Lakshmana have slashed off our sister Surpanakha's ears and nose," Ravana informed Mahiravan, "They have also invaded Lanka and killed Kumbhakarna and Indrajit." Ravana warned him that they are guarded by the powerful monkey Hanuman, and that Vibheeshan has also turned traitor and joined Rama's forces. Mahiravan assured Ravana that he would abduct the brothers and sacrifice them to Goddess Kali.

161 Mahiravan Learns About Hanuman

Mahiravan started planning how he would kidnap Rama and Lakshmana. He sent a spy to Rama's camp in Lanka to gather some useful information. Mahiravan's spy reported that Rama is guarded by Lakshmana at night. Hanuman protects him during the day but as he is asleep at night, his huge tail is coiled around the camp to protect it. His tail also serves as an umbrella to protect Rama from the sun and rain, and also serves as a fan and flag.

162 Mahiravan the Sorcerer

Mahiravan decided to steer clear of Hanuman when he heard of his prowess. Then, he was struck by a brilliant idea. *I shall take Vibheeshan's form and enter Rama's camp*, Mahiravan decided.Reaching Mount Suvela, he took the form of Vibheeshan and entered Rama's camp. The monkeys who were guarding the camp did not stop Mahiravan thinking he was Vibheeshan. Mahiravan thought, *The first part of my plan has worked. Now, it's time to set the second part into motion.* Using his powers of magic, Mahiravan released powerful fumes in the air that put the entire army of Rama to sleep.

Mahiravan quickly approached Rama's tent where he found Lakshmana unconscious on the ground outside. He entered the tent and picked up a sleeping Rama in his arms. Then, he exited the tent and picked up Lakshmana in his other hand.

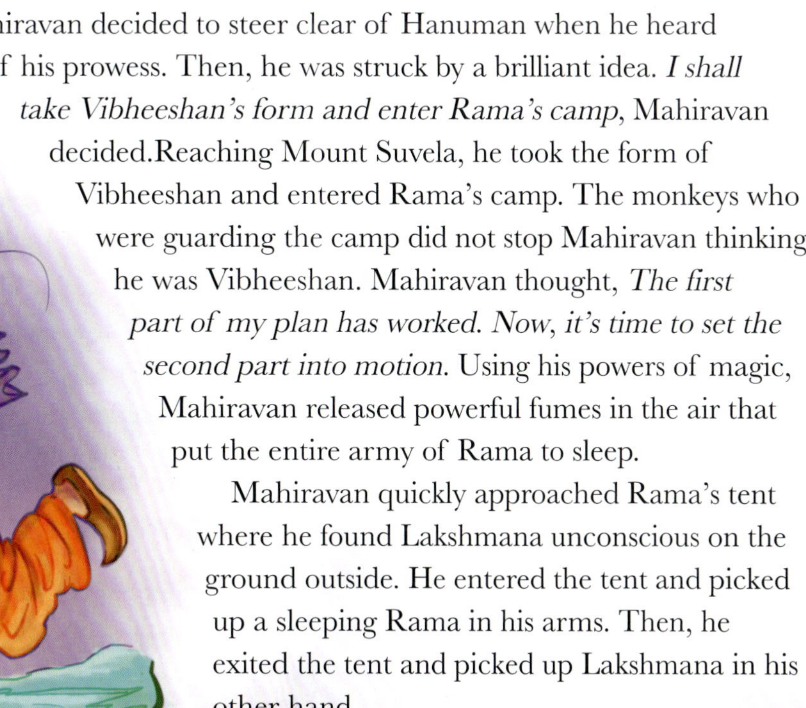

163 Rama and Lakshmana Kidnapped

Mahiravan knew that the effects of the spell would not last long and he would have to hurry up. He flew towards his kingdom in the netherworld with both the brothers. Hanuman was the first to recover from the powerful spell and his sixth instinct sensed that something was wrong. He rushed to Rama's tent where he found Rama and Lakshmana missing. Hanuman woke up Sugreev and Jambavan. Sugreev immediately sent the monkeys to look for them. But they couldn't be found anywhere. When he saw Vibheeshan, Hanuman rushed to give him the bad tidings.

Sugreev shouted. "Let us attack Lanka right now!" "They are not in Lanka," Vibheeshan replied. "I'm sure this has been done by Mahiravan."

164 Vibheeshan's Revelation

Vibheeshan informed Hanuman, Sugreev and Jambavan that he was sure that Rama and Lakshmana had been kidnapped by Ravana's brother Mahiravan, the lord of the netherworld upon the request of Ravana. "Ravana wants to eliminate Rama and Lakshmana at any cost after the death of Kumbhakarna and Indrajit," Vibheeshan revealed. "He has realised how powerful they are and has sought Mahiravan's help to take Rama and Lakshmana to Pataal Lok." Hanuman was concerned about what would happen to Rama and Lakshmana. Vibheeshan too was worried as he replied, "Mahiravan sacrifices all the enemies he captures to the Goddess Kali." Hanuman was calm and composed. "I shall not let any harm come to Lord Rama and Lakshmana!" he vowed.

165 Hanuman's Rescue Mission

Hanuman decided to travel all alone to the netherworld to rescue Rama and Lakshmana from the clutches of Mahiravan. He knew that only he would be able to withstand the illusion and sorcery of the demons in Pataal.

Vibheeshan guided him on the precautions he needed to take in the netherworld and warned him that his mission would be a dangerous one. Jambavan was confident that only Hanuman could rescue Lord Rama and Lakshmana since he had been blessed by the gods themselves to be invincible in battle.

166 Hanuman and the Birds

Hanuman quickly travelled to Pataal Lok. Once he reached there, he had no idea where to look for Rama and Lakshmana. He stopped to rest and think under the shade of a huge tree where he overheard two birds talking. Hanuman could understand the language of the birds.He found their conversation very interesting.

"Mahiravan has captured two princes and will offer them as a sacrifice to the Goddess Kali tomorrow morning. Let us fly to the palace now and wait for the feast to begin so we can get some food," one bird said to the other.

167 Hanuman's Son

As the birds flew away to Mahiravan's palace, Hanuman reduced his size to that of a small fly and followed them. After flying for a long time, they arrived at Mahiravan's palace. The birds sat on a nearby tree. Hanuman decided to enter the palace through the main gate. A fearsome creature who was guarding the gates of the palace, commanded Hanuman to stop. He was half-reptile and half-monkey. The creature stared at Hanuman in surprise and exclaimed, "You are a monkey!"

"Yes, I see that you too are half-monkey," an amused Hanuman replied. "What is your name?" The creature introduced himself as Makardhwaj, the son of the mighty Hanuman. Now, it was Hanuman's turn to be surprised. *How is it that he claims to be my son?* a perplexed Hanuman thought. *How is it that I have a son?*

168 Father and Son Meet

How is it possible that I have a son when I am not even married? Hanuman thought. Makardhwaj revealed that when his father Hanuman was returning after setting Lanka on fire, a drop of his perspiration fell into the sea and was swallowed by his reptile mother. This was why he was born as half-monkey and half-reptile. "But who are you and why have you come here? Outsiders are banned in Pataal Lok. Leave this place at once or I shall kill you." Hanuman assumed a gigantic size so that Makardhwaj recognised him at once. "Father!" he exclaimed, falling at Hanuman's feet. "I'm so happy to meet you, my son," Hanuman said, embracing Makardhwaj warmly.

169 Makardhwaj Helps Hanuman

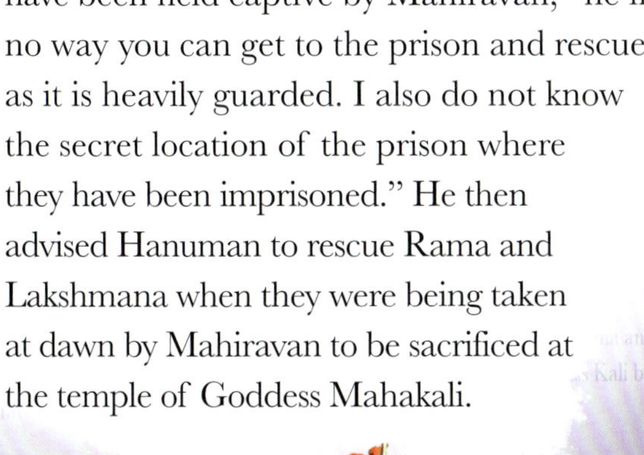

Makardhwaj prostrated himself before Hanuman and asked him to bless him. Hanuman told him the entire story of how Rama's army had gone to Lanka to rescue Sita from Ravana and how Mahiravana had abducted them. Makardhwaj then agreed to help his father. "Rama and Lakshmana have been held captive by Mahiravan," he informed. "There is no way you can get to the prison and rescue them as it is heavily guarded. I also do not know the secret location of the prison where they have been imprisoned." He then advised Hanuman to rescue Rama and Lakshmana when they were being taken at dawn by Mahiravan to be sacrificed at the temple of Goddess Mahakali.

170 Hanuman Fights Makardhwaj

Hanuman decided to wait till dawn to rescue Rama and Lakshmana. Makardhwaj bowed before him and said, "Father, I have done my duty as a son but now as a servant of Mahiravan I must fight you." Hanuman reminded him that Mahiravan was on the side of evil. But Mahiravan was adamant to prevent Hanuman from entering. Hanuman said, "You do your duty, as I do mine. May the one who is on the side of Dharma win this battle." There was a fierce battle and Makardhwaj was defeated. "I am proud to have a valiant son like you," Hanuman said as he proudly embraced his son.

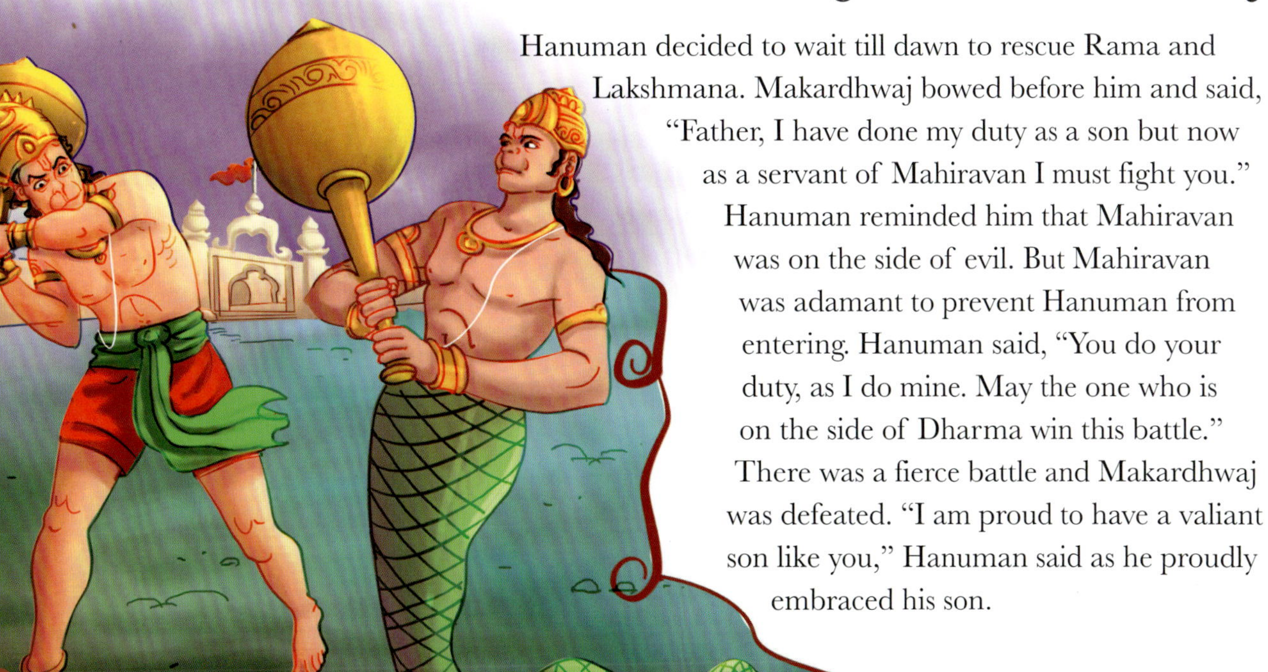

171 Mahiravan's Secret

After Hanuman defeated Makardhwaj in battle, Makardhwaj allowed him to enter Pataal Lok. He revealed the location of the temple where Rama and Lakshmana would be taken at the crack of dawn, and also the secret to kill Mahiravan. "He's a powerful sorcerer. In his temple there are five lamps kept in different directions. All these lamps must be extinguished at the same time to kill Mahiravan." Hanuman thanked Makardhwaj and said, "Remember that one is always rewarded for joining the forces of good."

172 Hanuman Meets Mahakali

Hanuman reached the heavily guarded temple. Reducing his size he prostrated himself before the idol of the goddess. "Jai Shri Ram," Hanuman chanted. "Jai Mahakali." Goddess Kali appeared and asked him what he wanted. "Please do not allow Mahiravan to sacrifice Lord Rama and Lakshmana before you," Hanuman pleaded. Mahakali initially expressed her helplessness since though Rama was an incarnation of the Lord, and Mahiravan was evil, yet he was also one of her greatest devotees. However, Mahakali assured to help him, "Now, listen to what I have to say very carefully!"

173 Hanuman's Plan

At dawn, Mahiravan entered the temple with Rama and Lakshmana. Hanuman had reduced his form so he was invisible. Now that he had found Rama not even Yamraj could stop him. But he remembered Mahakali's instructions. He flew towards Rama and Lakshmana and whispered something into their ears. Rama and Lakshmana smiled. *Hanuman never fails me*! Rama thought. Both of them nodded that they had understood what to do.

Mahiravan began worshipping Mahakali and placed offerings of food in front of the deity but the food started disappearing. Mahiravan thought that the goddess was accepting his offerings. Actually, it was Hanuman who was eating up all the food.

174 The Final Sacrifice

When all the food offered to Mahakali was consumed, Mahiravan ordered Rama and Lakshmana to kneel. He ordered his soldiers to chop off their heads as soon as they bowed to the goddess. Lakshmana thundered, "Don't you know that we are the royal princes of Ayodhya who never bow before anyone?" Mahiravan was furious but Rama calmed him down. "We don't know how to bow," Rama explained to Mahiravan. "Why don't you show us how to bow before the goddess? We shall follow your actions."

175 The Five Forms of Hanuman

Mahiravan laughed sarcastically when he learnt that Rama and Lakshmana did not know how to bow. Hanuman took his Panchamukha form with the heads of Garuda, Narasimha, Varaha, Hayagreeva and himself. Each head signified a particular trait. Hanuman's form displayed courage and strength, Narasimha's form showed fearlessness, Garuda's form had magical skills and the power to cure snake bites, Varaha's form indicated health and Hayagreeva's form meant victory over enemies. With these five heads, Hanuman blew at the five oil lamps that were kept in five directions inside the temple. As the five lamps were extinguished, Mahiravan's strength disappeared. Hanuman snatched the sword from an executioner and beheaded Mahiravan. "The sacrifice to Mahakali has been made!" Hanuman declared.

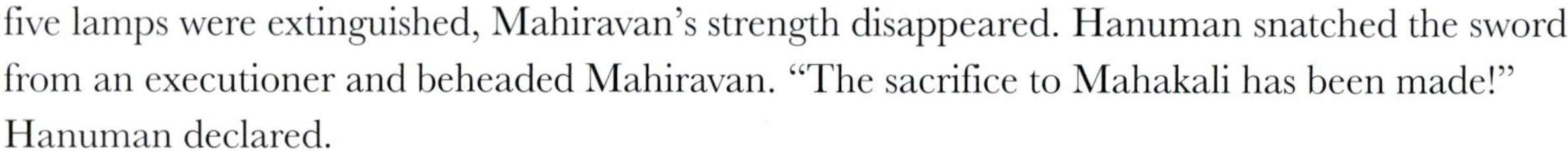

176 Kali's Boon

After Hanuman killed Mahiravan, he told Rama and Lakshmana about his son Makardhwaj and how he had helped him. Rama was very pleased with Makardhwaj and crowned him as the new king of Pataal Lok. Hanuman prayed to Mahakali and thanked her for helping him rescue Lord Rama and Lakshmana. Pleased by his devotion, Mahakali appeared and blessed Hanuman. "May my heart always be devoted to Lord Rama," Hanuman requested. "So be it!" a pleased Mahakali said. As a mark of his devotion she blessed him to be her dwara-paal or gatekeeper. Bhairava and Hanuman guard the two sides of the entrance of the temple that leads to goddess Kali's shrine.

177 Hanuman Returns to Lanka

After instructing Makardhwaj to always follow the path of righteousness, Hanuman left Pataal Lok. With Rama and Lakshmana on his shoulders, Hanuman flew back to their camp. Sugreev, Vibheeshan, Jambavan, Angad and the other warriors were overjoyed to see them back and praised Hanuman's devotion. Rama thanked Hanuman and said, "You are as dear to me as my brother Lakshmana."Lakshmana nodded his approval because there was none as mighty or devoted as the great Hanuman.

178 Ravana Summons Narantak

Ravana learnt that Hanuman had killed Mahiravan and rescued Rama and Lakshmana. He was very angry. His son Narantak was a powerful warrior with a huge demon army. He ordered his messenger Dhumketu to fly to Narantak and convey his message for help. Narantak immediately arrived in Lanka with his huge army. Ravana told him that Hanuman had killed many of his brothers, and also Mahiravan. "I want you to avenge their deaths by killing Hanuman," Ravana ordered Narantak.

179 Mandodari's Request

Ravana's queen Mandodari persuaded him to surrender to Rama and free Sita. "We have lost our most powerful son Indrajit. All your mighty warriors have died. I don't want to lose you as well." Ravana paid no heed to his wife's warnings. He would not accept defeat when his brother and sons had been killed. "You speak like the traitor Vibheeshan who has joined the enemy. Do you doubt your husband's power?"

He has lost all sense of reason because of his pride. Mandodari thought sadly. *I wonder how much humiliation we have to face at the hands of monkeys.*

180 Narantak Killed

Narantak and his army attacked the monkeys with great force. Narantak released his powerful arrows at Hanuman. But Hanuman grabbed his arrows and broke them on his thigh and broke Narantak's chariot into pieces. Narantak attacked Hanuman with his sword but Hanuman broke it into two with his mace. Narantak attacked Hanuman with his bare hands but Hanuman struck him a mighty blow on his chest. Hanuman picked Narantak up and lifted him above his head. Then, Hanuman spun him and flung him in the air. Narantak's army fled. "Jai Shri Ram!" Hanuman shouted. "Glory to Hanuman!" the monkeys shouted in reply.

181 Ravana's Thousand Warriors

Ravana's mighty warriors and generals had perished in the battle against Rama's army. He then summoned his army of the thousand immortal rakshasa warriors. Vibheeshan was worried and broke the news to Rama. Hanuman immediately offered to defeat the thousand rakshasas single-handedly. "But these warriors cannot be killed, Hanuman," Vibheeshan exclaimed. Even Rama expressed his doubts. But Jambavan was confident that Hanuman can make the impossible, possible.

"Don't worry, My Lord," Hanuman replied. "Have faith in your devotee."

182 Ravana's Warning

Ravana greeted his army of a thousand immortal warriors and advised them to beware of Hanuman. Ravana feared Hanuman the most in Rama's army after he had burnt down Lanka. In a hand-to-hand combat, Hanuman had struck Ravana a powerful blow that knocked him unconscious. Jambavan quickly stopped Hanuman, stating that Ravana was fated to die only at the hands of Lord Rama.

Ravana's thousand immortal demons were surprised when they saw a single monkey approaching them in the battlefield. They laughed at Hanuman when he approached them confidently, holding his mace.

183 Hanuman Challenges the Immortals

A terrible battle began between Hanuman and his thousand opponents. But even after Hanuman struck them unconscious, the demons revived to attack him. "You can't kill us, Hanuman," they shouted. "It is best you accept defeat and return to Rama to tell him about our powers."

"Of course, I will," Hanuman replied. "But I shall do that only after defeating you. Why don't all of you attack me at once to test my might? Then, you can go and tell the wicked Ravana all about it," he challenged.

184 The Victorious Hanuman

Hanuman grew to a gigantic size and binding the thousand immortal demons with his tail, swung it with such force that they flew right into space, beyond the gravitational forces. Being immortal, they did not die, but their bodies dried up with lack of air, water and food as they roamed about in space helplessly.

Hanuman returned to his camp amid cheers from his companions. "I have sent them up," Hanuman declared as he bowed to Rama. "Since they are immortal, I've sent them to space from where they can never return." Rama embraced him.

185 Ravana's Ritual

Ravana realised that he would have to go to the battlefield himself. *Let me make myself invincible before I meet Rama in battle*, he thought.

He mounted his flying chariot and rose to the skies. With his divine powers he overpowered and captured the nine planets in chains and herded them back to Lanka. He began the sacrificial rituals to force the nine planets to realign in his favour. *Once I can control my own destiny, no one will be able to kill me on the battlefield*, he thought. Vibheeshan's spies reported to him about Ravana's sacrificial ritual. When Rama heard this, he held a meeting with Sugreev, Lakshman, Vibheeshan and his generals.

It was decided that Hanuman and Angad would lead a team of daredevil monkeys to Ravana's sacrificial hall, disrupt the proceedings and ensure that Ravana was unable to finish the sacrifice that gave him the power to change his destiny.

186 Hanuman Disrupts Ravana's Ritual

Hanuman, Angad and their band of monkeys arrived at the sacrificial hall where Ravana was meditating beside an altar of fire with all the planets chained before him. The band of monkeys rushed inside. Ravana was oblivious to this unwanted intrusion as he quietly chanted the mantras with his eyes closed. Hanuman blew out the sacrificial fire and Angad kicked away the ceremonial utensils. Still, Ravana did not stir. Hanuman ordered the monkeys to wipe off the occult diagrams or yantras painted on the floor. But even this did not rouse Ravana from his deep trance as he continued chanting his divine mantras. Hanuman said, "We have to stop Ravana from succeeding in changing the course of destiny." Angad said that he had a plan.

187 Angad's Mischievous Plan

Angad shared his mischievous plan with Hanuman who did not agree with it initially. But Hanuman finally relented as he had no other option. It was decided that Hanuman would keep the forces of Ravana at bay who had started arriving in large numbers while Angad and his team of monkeys would execute the plan.

"Enter the female chambers in the palace and scare away Ravana's wives to bring them here," Angad ordered his monkeys as Hanuman started fighting the demons who attacked them. The monkeys entered the female chambers and scared away Ravana's many wives to bring them to the sacrificial hall.

"Save us, my lord," Ravana's queens and concubines shouted to Ravana as the monkeys started pulling their hair and scratching their faces to break Ravana's concentration. But Ravana did not react or stir. Finally, Angad dragged Ravana's chief queen Mandodari to the sacrificial hall. The monkeys started scaring Mandodari as they bared their teeth, beat their chests and began to grunt menacingly.

Terrified, Mandodari lamented, "The day that I feared has finally arrived."

188 Ravana's Ritual Disrupted

Ravana continued to chant his mantras with his eyes closed as the monkeys scared his wife Mandodari. "My husband continues to meditate while monkeys threaten his wife's chastity," she cried angrily. "I have to face this humiliation because of your actions and you refuse to protect me!"

Mandodari's words put Ravana to shame. Enraged, he attacked the monkeys. Hanuman was elated that their plan had succeeded and Ravana's meditation had been disrupted. As Angad fought with Ravana, Hanuman rushed to free the planets imprisoned by Ravana. Angad stopped fighting with Ravana and fled.

Hanuman won the eternal gratitude of the planets for having freed them. It is believed that he exercises considerable power over them as a result. Hanuman's devotees worship him whenever faced with unfavourable astrological problems because of the configuration of the planets.

189 Hanuman Rescues Shani

When Ravana captured the nine planets, all of them accepted defeat except Shani. A furious Ravana ordered his men to hang him upside down and flog him. Then he left to perform his holy ritual. When Hanuman and his team spoiled Ravana's ritual and freed all the planets, they noticed that Shani was missing. When they located Shani he was in extreme pain because of the beatings. Hanuman rubbed oil all over his body and gave him a good massage. This lessened Shani's pain and he promised Hanuman that he would always protect whoever offers oil while worshipping him.From that day onwards, devotees always offer oil while praying to Shanidev.

190 Rama Faces Ravana

Before entering the battlefield, both Rama and Ravana prayed to Lord Shiva for victory. Rama rode to the battlefield in a royal chariot gifted to him by Indra. The gods stopped everything to watch the final battle between Rama and Ravana. As their chariots faced each other, Rama remembered how Ravana had carried away the defenceless Sita. Ravana remembered that his sister Soorpanakha had been insulted and his brothers were killed by Rama. "You shall die today, Rama," he thundered, releasing a powerful arrow.

191 Rama Fights Ravana

A terrible combat ensued between Rama and Ravana. Rama began to get frustrated. Every time his arrow severed an arm or head of Ravana, another head or arm grew back to replace it. Rama was worried as Ravana had inflicted heavy casualties on the monkey army. Lakshmana, Hanuman, Sugreev, Angad and Jambavan had all failed to kill Ravana. Ravana appeared to be invincible.

"My Lord, let us consult Vibheeshan," Hanuman suggested to Rama. "He must be aware of the secret to kill Ravana."

192 Another Mission for Hanuman

Rama met Vibheeshan and asked him to suggest a way to kill the invincible Ravana. Vibheeshan disclosed that Ravana had Shiva's divine bow. He had given that bow to his favourite queen Mandodari for safekeeping. Only she knew its exact location but it was certainly somewhere in her chambers. When the question arose as to who would get the bow from Mandodari's chambers, all eyes turned towards Hanuman. As soon as Rama nodded, Hanuman immediately transformed into the guise of a learned sage. Rama blessed Hanuman to be victorious and said, "I am sure you have thought of a way already while all of us are still thinking about the problem."

193 Hanuman Goes to Mandodari

Disguised as a sage, Hanuman entered Mandodari's chamber and told her that he had come from the Himalayas. "Lord Shiva told me that he has gifted Ravana a divine bow which is now with you. He has given me this holy water to spray on the bow," he said. Mandodari was reluctant. Offended, the sage got up to go, leaving the food and threatened, "Your husband will lose all his powers if the bow is not purified."

A scared Mandodari pleaded, "Don't be angry, holy one. Please wait while I fetch the bow."

194 Mandodari's Curse

When Mandodari returned with the bow, Hanuman pretended to chant holy mantras as he sprinkled some water on it. When Mandodari asked him to return the bow, Hanuman refused. "I cannot return this bow to you," he said, revealing his true form. "I apologise for deceiving you but I had no other choice. I must hand over this bow to Lord Rama and Ravana must pay for his sins."Just as Hanuman was about to leave with the bow, the furious Mandodari cursed him, "Just as I shall live in grief after my husband's death, you shall live forever, but separated from your Lord Rama."

195 Rama Assures Hanuman

When Hanuman returned with the bow, he told Rama of Mandodari's curse. Rama said, "The soul may leave the body, but we shall be together forever even after we die. I shall visit you in another incarnation." Hanuman understood the depth of Rama's words and bowed before him. Rama added, "I'm incomplete without you. Why do I rely only on you whenever I need help? No power can separate us!"

Rama examined Shiva's bow, and declared, "I shall put an end to Ravana's life with this bow tomorrow with the blessings of Lord Shiva."

196 Ravana Is Dead

Vibheeshan advised Rama, "Now that you have Shiva's bow with you, Ravana's death is certain. But aim your arrow at Ravana's navel where he has stored the nectar of immortality." Ravana and Rama were soon engaged in a deadly duel. Rama invoked the Brahmastra and aimed it at Ravana's navel. The arrow pierced Ravana's navel and squeezed out the nectar. Ravana fell dead on the ground.

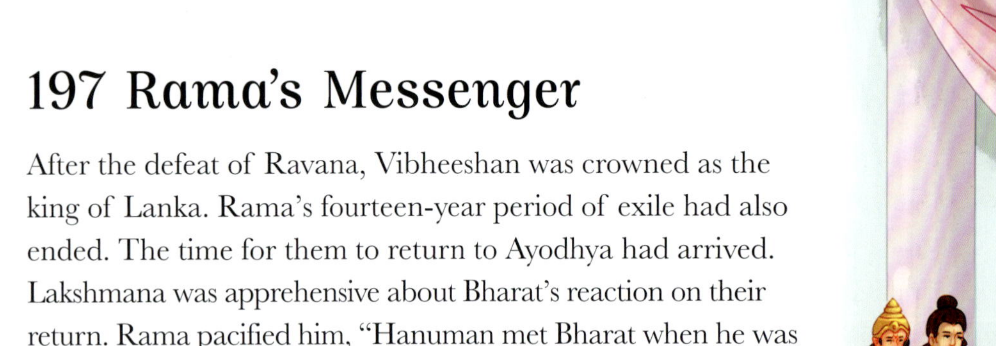

197 Rama's Messenger

After the defeat of Ravana, Vibheeshan was crowned as the king of Lanka. Rama's fourteen-year period of exile had also ended. The time for them to return to Ayodhya had arrived. Lakshmana was apprehensive about Bharat's reaction on their return. Rama pacified him, "Hanuman met Bharat when he was flying here with the mountain to cure you. Bharat and Shatrughna are more than anxious for our return to Ayodhya. But I still wish to inform Bharat of our return."

"Let us send Hanuman ahead of us to Ayodhya to break the news to Bharat," Lakshmana suggested. Hanuman was summoned and given the responsibility of going in disguise as Rama's messenger to Ayodhya.

198 Hanuman Meets Bharat

Hanuman flew to Ayodhya disguised as a brahmin. He observed that the people of Ayodhya were happy, safe and prosperous under Bharat's rule, yet there was a sadness in the air. The people were missing Rama, Sita and Lakshmana.

"Rama is our real king," a woman stated. "Bharat is just ruling on his behalf. We shall not be happy till Rama returns to Ayodhya." Another man seconded her, "The light has gone from our lives. We pray that Rama returns to Ayodhya soon." Everywhere Hanuman went in Ayodhya, he was greeted by the same sentiments. *There is so much love and respect for Lord Rama,* Hanuman thought. *Now, let me approach Bharat.*

Hanuman went to Bharat's palace disguised as a brahmin and informed him about Rama's victory over Ravana. Bharat was overjoyed and this joy turned to elation when he heard that Rama, Lakshmana and Sita were returning home to Ayodhya.

199 Hanuman Returns

Seeing Bharat's happiness over the news that Rama, Lakshmana and Sita were returning to Ayodhya, Hanuman was relieved. Hanuman then revealed his true form to Bharat who embraced Hanuman warmly and ordered decorations, music, dance and celebrations to be held to welcome Rama, Lakshmana and Sita.

Hanuman took leave of Bharat and took a mighty leap to return to Lanka again. He told Rama how everyone in Ayodhya, including Bharat, were eagerly waiting to receive him as their king. Meanwhile, the news of Rama's return revived the spirits of the people of Ayodhya and they celebrated on the streets to welcome Rama, Sita and Lakshmana.

200 Flight to Ayodhya

It was decided that Rama, Sita and Lakshmana would be accompanied by the main allies who would travel to Ayodhya first. The rest of the army would arrive on foot later to attend Rama's coronation ceremony. Vibheeshan, who would also travel to Ayodhya with Lord Rama, offered the services of his aerial chariot or the Pushpaka Vimana.

Rama, Lakshmana, Sita, Hanuman, Vibheeshan, Sugreev, Angad and Jambavan boarded the Pushpaka Vimana which flew off to Ayodhya. As they were airborne, Rama looked at Hanuman and felt very grateful for all the services that Hanuman had rendered to him.He took off the ring in his right hand and handed it over to Hanuman. "Here, Hanuman," Rama said. "I want you to have my ring!"

201 Hanuman Explains His Action

Pleased with Hanuman's devotion, Rama gifted him his ring as they flew over the ocean towards Ayodhya. Hanuman took the ring and examined it closely. He appeared surprised as he turned the ring in his hand over and over. Then, he squeezed the ring with his strong fingers and bit it with his teeth. Everyone in the flying chariot was surprised. But they were shocked when Hanuman tossed the ring over the side of the flying chariot and it fell straight into the ocean.

"Oh no!" Vibheeshan exclaimed. "What did you do Hanuman? I thought you were the greatest devotee of Lord Rama. But this action was not befitting someone like you. How could you throw away Lord Rama's gift into the water?"

Hanuman turned to Vibheeshan and replied, "My dear friend, tell me of what value is that ring to me? It doesn't have the name of Lord Rama inscribed upon it. Neither does it have Lord Rama's name within its hard exterior. I bit the ring to check that as well."

202 Vibheeshan's Query

Vibheeshan was not satisfied with Hanuman's explanation that he had thrown away Lord Rama's ring just because it did not have his name written on it. Hanuman saw the astounded look on Vibheeshan's face and explained further, "I want only the things that are real and are of practical use to me. I decided that the ring was useless for me and hence, I got rid of it."

Vibheeshan was stunned at Hanuman's reasoning.

"Please allow me to ask you a question, Hanuman," a confused Vibheeshan stated. "You are the greatest warrior whom I have ever seen and there is no doubt about your unparalleled devotion to Lord Rama which cannot be questioned. When I think about the great acts that you have performed in the service of Lord Rama, my head still reels. My heart is full of the bliss of devotion when I recall the great acts of service that you have performed for Lord Rama that no one else could perform. Then why, O great Hanuman, won't you accept anything that doesn't have the name Rama inscribed upon it? Isn't it enough that the gift is from Lord Rama himself ?"

In reply, Hanuman just smiled at Vibheeshan.

203 Hanuman Opens Up His Chest

When he saw Hanuman smiling, Vibheeshan said, "Lord Rama's name is not inscribed on your body either. Go and jump into the ocean as well." Hanuman ripped open his chest to reveal Lord Rama and Sita shining in their glory.

"O great devotee," Vibheeshan cried out. "Forgive me for doubting your devotion. I am blessed as I have never seen the glory of God on any devotee like I see on you."

204 Hanuman Dives into the Ocean

Even Rama and Sita were awestruck by Hanuman's wonderful display of devotion. Rama smiled at his greatest devotee and said, "You have thrown my ring into the ocean. Please bring it back to me!"

To help Hanuman find that small ring, Vibheeshan decided to make his task easier. He ordered the flying chariot to be taken close to the spot where Hanuman had cast the ring into the ocean, and halted the chariot there in mid-air. Hanuman chanted Lord Rama's name and dived into the ocean below. Everyone thought it was an impossible task. "If anyone can find that ring," Jambavan stated with quiet optimism, "It's Hanuman."

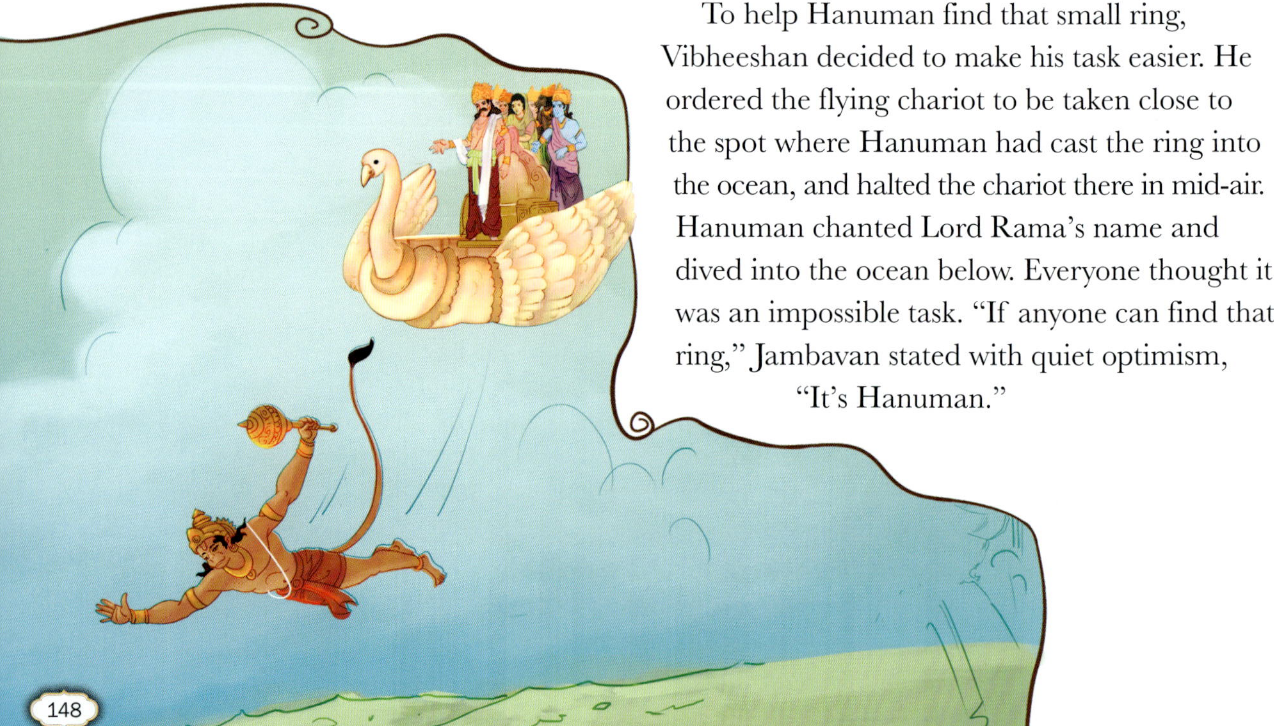

205 Hanuman Meets an Ancient Sage

Hanuman reached a mountain range where an old sage sat in a state of deep meditation (samadhi). "Welcome, O son of Vayu and devotee of Lord Rama," the sage greeted Hanuman. Hanuman was surprised that the sage knew who he was.

"Although I sit here beneath the ocean, I know what is going on in this world thanks to the power of my meditation," the sage explained. "You come at the command of Lord Rama to retrieve his ring that you threw away from the Pushpaka Vimana." *This divine sage can help me find Lord Rama's ring*, Hanuman thought happily.

206 The Mountain of Rings

Hanuman respectfully asked the sage where the ring was. The sage replied, "In life, everything is revealed to those who are observant." Hanuman stared at the valleys and smaller hills that surrounded the mountain that the sage was seated on. Then, he noticed that the sage was sitting on an entire mountain made out of rings. Hanuman thought, *All the rings look just like Lord Rama's ring which I had thrown into the ocean.*

Hanuman bowed to the sage and humbly asked, "O great one, how do I know which one of these rings belongs to Lord Rama?"

207 The Secret of the Rings

The sage told a puzzled Hanuman, "In countless incarnations, you have served as the devotee of Lord Rama, helped good win over evil and bared your heart to Vibheeshan; in each life you have thrown these rings in the ocean at the precise spot creating this mountain of rings over which I am meditating, have come looking for it, and I have helped you each time. I have seen you many times before this, in different incarnations. Sitting here meditating since the beginning of the Universe, the way and play of the Lord has been my only delight."

208 Hanuman Returns

Hanuman was struck speechless at the sage's story. "Take any ring from here as they all belong to Lord Rama," the sage told him. Hanuman looked around and with a joyous shout recognised the ring he was looking for. It was lying at the feet of the sage.

With the ring safely with him, Hanuman travelled at great speed towards the Pushpaka chariot where everyone awaited him. As Hanuman handed the ring to Rama, their eyes met. Both smiled.

209 The Feast of the Monkeys

When they reached Ayodhya on the Pushpak Vimana, Rama received a rousing welcome by the people. The kingdom had been decorated with festoons and lamps glittered the whole city. That occasion is still celebrated even today as Diwali. Soon, the army that had led Rama to victory also arrived for Rama's coronation.

"I wish to hold a feast for the entire monkey brigade before they leave for Kishkindha," Rama ordered that the arrangements for a fine feast be made. The feast was spectacular and the choicest of delicacies and fruits were served to the monkeys. Rama, Sita, Lakshmana, Bharat and Shatrughna personally went around ensuring that all the monkeys were served well and ate to their heart's content.

Suddenly, a monkey jumped up high in the air. Another monkey followed him and soon, another followed. To Rama's surprise, Hanuman too, jumped high up in the air. Everybody was happy that the monkeys were jumping about. It showed that they were pleased with the feast.

210 The Jumping Monkeys

Rama was surprised when he saw the monkeys jumping in the air one after the other.

"I am glad that you are enjoying the food," Rama said to Hanuman. "But tell me, is that the real reason for your jumping up in such joy?"

Hanuman looked sheepish after Rama asked him this question.

"My Lord, I must confess that I had no great reason to jump in the air," Hanuman confessed.

"Oh!" Rama exclaimed. "I hope the food is good enough."

"The food is delicious, My Lord," Hanuman assured Rama. "Actually, I jumped because the monkey seated next to me jumped. I jumped just to show him that I could jump higher than him."

Rama was speechless for a while.

"But why did the monkey next to you jump?" Rama asked Hanuman.

"Well, he jumped because the monkey seated next to him jumped, and he wanted to show him that he could jump higher!" Hanuman explained. Now, Rama's curiosity was fully aroused.

I must find out why the first monkey jumped, Rama thought to himself.

211 The Monkey and the Banana

Accompanied by Hanuman, Rama went to enquire why the monkeys had jumped. It was revealed that a small monkey had jumped first, and others had followed. Rama gently asked him why he had jumped. "While peeling a banana, it slipped out of my hand and jumped in the air. I wanted to show that I can jump higher." Hanuman explained, "The monkey seated next to him thought that he was challenging him and jumped higher. Soon, everyone challenged each other!"

212 Sugreev's Worry

Rama planned to host another feast after his coronation. Sugreev was concerned. His monkeys lived in the jungle and lacked social graces. Sugreev addressed them, "The people of Ayodhya should not think that we monkeys lack social graces." All the monkeys promised to behave. But one monkey addressed Sugreev worriedly, "My lord, we monkeys might make mistakes. Someone should be there to monitor us so that we don't go wrong."

213 Hanuman's Dilemma

Sugreev appointed Hanuman to take charge of the monkeys. When they were all seated to his satisfaction, Hanuman approached Rama to pay his respects. Rama lovingly requested, "Please sit with me and have your meal."

Hanuman was in a dilemma. *How can I eat with Lord Rama who is my master*? Hanuman wondered.

214 Rama Invites Hanuman to Share Food

When Rama invited him to have food with him, Hanuman was in a dilemma. He did not think it was proper for a devotee to eat with Rama. He replied, "I shall eat later as there is no place reserved for me now, and neither is there a plate served." Rama guessed what was going on in Hanuman's mind. "Don't worry, Hanuman," Rama smiled and said gently. "Come and sit beside me!" Using his divine powers, Rama created enough space beside him for Hanuman to sit.

For someone who has created so much space in the world, it is so easy to create a little more space! Hanuman thought as he sat beside Rama. Rama insisted that Hanuman eat from his plate. "You are as dear to me as a younger brother and best friend, Hanuman," Rama said. "Please eat from my plate as we are one and the same."

215 Hanuman Remains in Ayodhya

After Rama's coronation, Hanuman decided to stay back in Ayodhya to serve Rama. Though they were sad to be parted from him, Sugreev, Angad and Jambavan left for Kishkindha. "Your destiny is to serve Lord Rama," Sugreev said as he embraced Hanuman.

Hanuman served Rama eagerly and left no task for the others. Lakshmana, Bharat and Shatrughna felt that they were unable to serve Rama as everything was being done by Hanuman. They decided to ask Sita to solve this problem. Sita was willing to help them as Hanuman was not letting even her to serve her husband.

216 The Schedule of Services

Sita with Lakshmana, Bharata, Shatrughna prepared a schedule for the services offered to Rama from morning to night. Hanuman was excluded from any service in the schedule. These were equally divided between Sita, Lakshmana, Bharat and Shatrughna. Sita went to take Rama's approval for the schedule.

"Please approve this schedule, My Lord," Sita said as she handed over the list to Rama. Rama went through the schedule and smiled when he realised that no service had been allotted to his favourite devotee Hanuman.

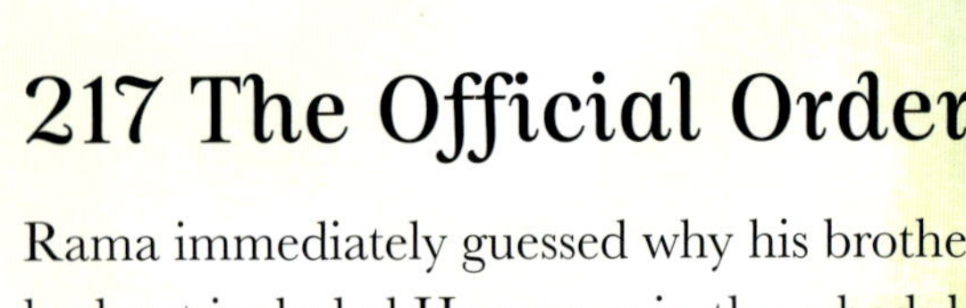

217 The Official Order

Rama immediately guessed why his brothers and his wife had not included Hanuman in the schedule of services. He did not say a word even though Hanuman's total exclusion from the schedule was not fair. *They have made this decision out of their love for me and not because of their dislike for Hanuman*, he thought. *Let's see how Hanuman tackles this problem.*

Upon Sita's request, Rama fixed his seal on the schedule to make it an official order. Hanuman, who was unaware of the happenings, arrived the next day to enter Rama's room to press his feet. But he was stopped by Shatrughna.

"Stop, Hanuman," Shatrughna ordered. "This service has been allotted to me now!"

218 The Yawning Service

Hanuman became very sad when he learned that he had been denied of all opportunities to serve Rama. He approached Lakshmana. "Is there any service that I may offer to Lord Rama?" he asked him.

"You may take up any service that is not mentioned in the list," Lakshmana replied. *There is no possible service left for Hanuman to render to Rama*, Lakshmana thought confidently. *All the services have been divided among us.* "I shall take up the yawning service for Lord Rama. When he yawns, I shall snap my fingers to protect him from evil effects," Hanuman said.

Lakshmana consulted Bharat, Shatrughna and Sita who agreed to let Hanuman do the yawning service.

219 Hanuman Always with Rama

Lakshmana, Sita, Bharat and Shatrughna were unaware of the nature of the yawning service and hence they agreed to it. This service required Hanuman to always be present with Rama. He was always on the alert to snap his fingers whenever Rama yawned. Rama's brothers and Sita were completely stunned. Rama smiled at their discomfort. *Not even all their combined intelligence could equal Hanuman's intelligence*, he thought.

It was just a bit too much when Hanuman followed Rama into his bedroom at night. Sita ordered him to stop. "But Sita Mata," Hanuman protested. "The yawning service is required most during the night when Lord Rama sleeps so that he has a restful night."

220 Rama's Yawns Don't Stop

Sita stopped Hanuman when he tried to enter Rama's bedroom. But Hanuman insisted on performing his yawning service. Rama gently ordered Hanuman to go and rest for the night. Hanuman had no other option but to retreat.

I have to continue my yawning service as this is the only way I can serve Lord Rama, Hanuman thought. He climbed up to Rama's bedroom balcony and started snapping his fingers as he chanted Lord Rama's name. Soon, Sita was alarmed with Rama's repeated yawns. She ran to fetch Lakshmana, Bharat and Shatrughna who were all greatly concerned at Rama's state. They sought the advice of Sage Vashishtha who was present in the palace. He immediately guessed what had happened, thanks to his divine powers.

221 Sage Vashishtha's Logic

Sage Vashishtha said, "Find Hanuman immediately." After a long search, Hanuman was found on the balcony, chanting Rama's name and snapping his fingers. When Hanuman saw Rama's condition, he stopped snapping his fingers. Rama stopped yawning immediately.

"Hanuman is the greatest devotee of Rama and also the purest," Sage Vashishtha said. "Rama wanted to accept the services of Hanuman. It was not Hanuman's snap for Rama's yawn but Rama's yawn for Hanuman's snap. Lord Rama reciprocates to his greatest devotee's love." Sita, Lakshman, Bharat and Shatrughna realised Hanuman's determination and promised that they would never interfere in Hanuman's service to Lord Rama.

222 The Colour of the Flowers

Once, Rama was seated in his court. "Do you remember the colour of the flowers in Ashok Vatika?" Rama asked Sita. Sita replied that the flowers were white. Hanuman interrupted, "No. The flowers were red in colour." Sita protested. "I cannot be wrong as I was in Ashok Vatika for a month while you were there for a few hours." Hanuman insisted that there were only red flowers there. "Both of you are right," Rama replied."You were always in a state of meditation in Ashok Vatika," Rama explained to Sita. "Your mind was pure and you saw everything white, including the flowers. But Hanuman was very angry with Ravana. Forget the flowers , he saw everything else in Lanka also as red because of his anger."

223 Narada Tests Hanuman

Once, Narada arrived in Ayodhya. Seeing Hanuman's devotion for Lord Rama, Narada decided to test him. He wanted Hanuman himself to tell about his devotion.

"Hanuman, you are not a true devotee of Rama," Narada said. "According to the Vedas, such is the gravity of the sin of the person who sets fire to another person's house that no sin is incurred even if someone kills that person. When you went to Lanka to find Sita, you did not set fire to just one house. You set fire to many houses of the rakshasas. How can you claim to be a devotee of the Lord after indulging in such a sin?" Narada demanded. The intelligent Hanuman realised that Narada was trying to test his devotion for Lord Rama and smiled.

224 Why Hanuman Burnt Lanka

Narada questioned Hanuman about how he could still call himself a devotee of Rama after having burnt the rakshasas in Lanka. Hanuman replied, "One of the most important duties of a Rama Bhakt is to perform the final rites of dead bodies so that they attain a better life in their next birth." A surprised Narada then said, "But the rakshasas were alive, not dead bodies."

"In Lanka, no one, except my friend Vibheeshan, was chanting the name of Lord Rama," Hanuman explained. "Our Shastras mention that those who do not chant Lord Rama's holy name are as good as dead. So I burnt the rakshasas along with their belongings to free them of their miserable existence."

225 Hanuman Explains His Actions

Narada was curious to know why Hanuman had killed only some rakshasas and spared the rest. Hanuman replied, "I have killed the most evil ones. Many rakshasa warriors also died fighting Lord Rama's army. The rakshasas who remained alive shall mend their ways under Vibheeshan, a great devotee of Lord Rama." Narada then asked, "Why did you let out such a loud roar after you set fire to the houses in Lanka? Many pregnant rakshasis feared that the babies in their wombs would get aborted." Hanuman explained that the roar was a warning to the surviving rakshasas not to trudge the path of evil. The babies who died in the womb would have grown up to be evil and disturbed the peace of this earth." A pleased Narada hugged and praised Hanuman for his unrivalled devotion to Rama.

226 Rama's Dilemma

One day, Sage Vishwamitra arrived at Rama's court. He was angry that he had been insulted by Yayati, the king of Kasi and wanted Rama to avenge his insult.

"But I have never heard of Yayati disrespecting anyone," Rama exclaimed in surprise. Vishwamitra exclaimed angrily, "You must kill him if you are a true disciple of mine." Rama knew that he had no other choice but to kill Yayati. In those days, it was a king's duty to obey his Guru's command.

Oh, what a strange dilemma I am in, Rama thought. *On one hand, I have to follow my Guru's orders. But if I kill Yayati, I lose a good friend and his people lose a good king.*

227 Narada's Plan to Test Rama

Rama's Guru Vishwamitra claimed to be insulted by Yayati and asked Rama to kill him. This was part of a plan hatched by Narada after the celestial sages were divided in their opinion regarding Rama's divinity. One group believed that Rama was supreme while the other group thought that the Lord's name was above Rama himself. Then Narada came up with this clever plan. Vishwamitra was chosen to execute the first part.

"Vishwamitra must ask Rama to kill Yayati," Narada explained his plan. "This will be Rama's test as he will be caught between killing his friend and obeying his Guru."

"But what about the Lord's name?" Sage Agastya enquired.

"That will be decided later. Hanuman, the greatest devotee of Rama, will be tested to prove this," Narada replied.

228 Yayati Offends Vishwamitra

After Vishwamitra ordered him to kill Yayati, Rama was in a moral dilemma. Vishwamitra explained how Yayati had insulted him. "A few days ago, some of Yayati's subjects complained to him about wild elephants destroying their crops and terrorising them. As it was his duty as a king to protect his subjects, Yayati went to the forest to hunt down the elephants. He was so engrossed in trapping the wild elephants that he didn't notice me as I approached him. I tried to attract his attention but he did not pay his respects to me and has insulted me. That is why you have to kill Yayati to avenge my insult, Rama," Vishwamitra ordered.

Rama was puzzled. *How can my Guru be angry with Yayati for such a small offence?* he wondered. *But I have no choice but to obey him.* Rama decided to send a messenger to Kasi immediately, declaring war against Yayati.

229 Yayati Rushes to Ayodhya

Rama's messenger arrived in Kasi and broke the news that Rama would be attacking soon. *But what have I done to earn Lord Rama's displeasure?* a bewildered Yayati thought. *My entire family, including my wife Yashodhara and my children are all devotees of Lord Rama. I must rush to Ayodhya immediately and beg for Rama's forgiveness.*

Just as Yayati was preparing to ride to Ayodhya, Narada arrived. Yayati greeted him respectfully. "Why do you look so troubled, King Yayati?" Narada asked. A worried Yayati explained that he was going to Ayodhya to meet Lord Rama to find out why he had declared war against him.

"Don't go to Ayodhya now," Narada advised Yayati. "Rama has given his word to Sage Vishwamitra that he will kill you. As we all know, Rama is always true to his word more than anything else."

230 Yayati Visits Anjana

Narada advised Yayati that Rama would kill him if he went to Ayodhya. Yayati said that he would apologise to Sage Vishwamitra whom he had unknowingly offended. Narada now put the second part of his plan into motion. "Only Hanuman can protect you from Rama. Seek the help of Devi Anjana, who is Hanuman's mother." Yayati reached Mount Kanchan where Devi Anjana was in deep meditation. "Please help me, Devi," he pleaded. Anjana was distracted from her meditation and opened her eyes to see Yayati at her feet.

231 Yayati Meets Hanuman

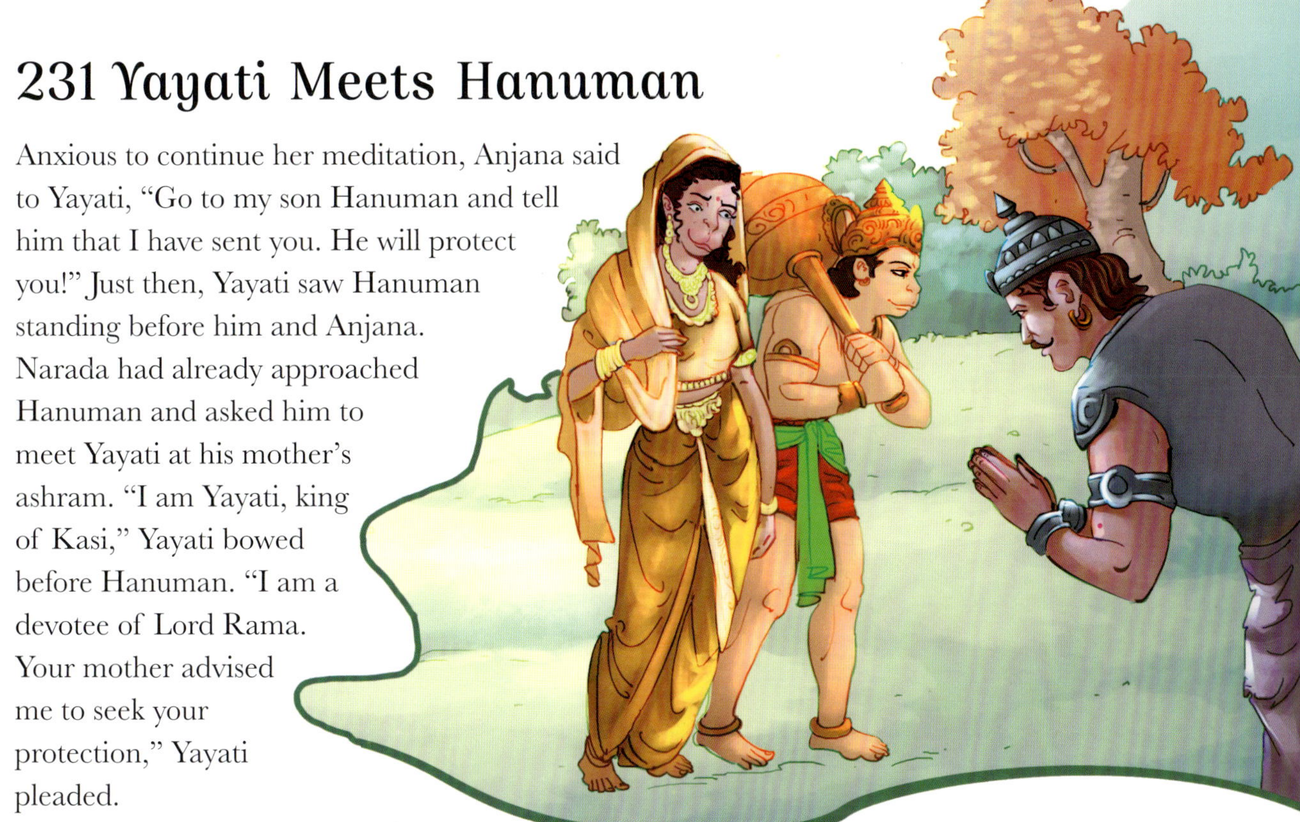

Anxious to continue her meditation, Anjana said to Yayati, "Go to my son Hanuman and tell him that I have sent you. He will protect you!" Just then, Yayati saw Hanuman standing before him and Anjana. Narada had already approached Hanuman and asked him to meet Yayati at his mother's ashram. "I am Yayati, king of Kasi," Yayati bowed before Hanuman. "I am a devotee of Lord Rama. Your mother advised me to seek your protection," Yayati pleaded.

Hanuman assured him, "If my mother has given you her word, it is my duty to protect you. Anjana and Hanuman had no idea that the threat to Yayati's life came from Rama himself.

232 Hanuman's Protection to Yayati

Yayati was relieved as he was now assured of Hanuman's protection. "I must have unknowingly done something to incur Sage Vishwamitra's displeasure," he explained to Hanuman. "He has asked Lord Rama to kill me. As Lord Rama cannot disobey his Guru, he has agreed." Anjana was angry. "I did not know that Lord Rama wants to kill you. I should not have promised you Hanuman's protection without hearing your full story. How can Hanuman fight against Lord Rama? I have to take back my promise!"

Hanuman intervened. "Lord Rama has taught me that it's our duty to help those who seek our protection. I shall protect King Yayati from any kind of danger even if his enemy is Lord Rama himself."

233 Hanuman's Request to Rama

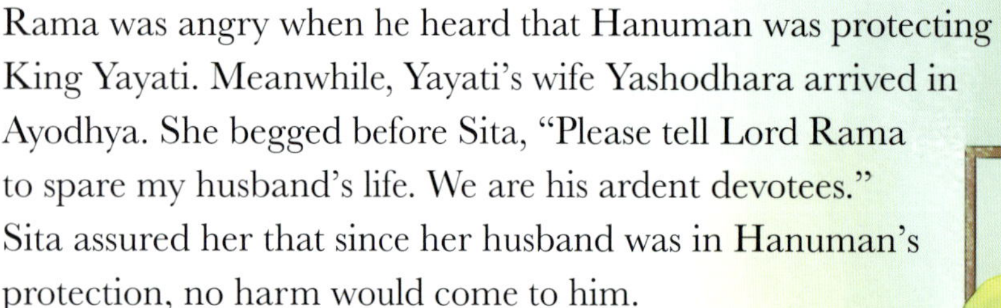

Rama was angry when he heard that Hanuman was protecting King Yayati. Meanwhile, Yayati's wife Yashodhara arrived in Ayodhya. She begged before Sita, "Please tell Lord Rama to spare my husband's life. We are his ardent devotees." Sita assured her that since her husband was in Hanuman's protection, no harm would come to him.

Rama reached Kasi with his brothers Lakshmana, Bharat and Shatrughna. Hanuman fell at Rama's feet when he was about to enter Kasi. "My Lord, have pity on your devotee Yayati and spare his life," he requested. "He's innocent."

234 Rama Stops Hanuman

Hanuman tried his best to persuade Rama not to kill Yayati. "I have to keep the promise made to my Guru," Rama said. He pushed Hanuman to one side. "I have to fulfill the promise made by my mother to protect Yayati," Hanuman said to Rama and refused to move. Rama demanded, "Hand over Yayati to me. I do not wish to fight you." Hanuman tried to convince Rama that Yayati was innocent. "I'm afraid there is no other way, Hanuman," Rama replied. "Yayati must die at my hands!" "If you wish to kill Yayati, you have to kill me first, My Lord," Hanuman said sadly as he assumed a huge form to bow before Rama.

235 Rama versus Hanuman

Thinking that Hanuman intended to fight him, Rama exclaimed, "Are you threatening me with your powers, Hanuman?" Hanuman replied humbly, "How can I threaten you? All the powers that I possess are only because of your blessings." But Hanuman refused to move from Rama's way and stood there like a mountain. He had vowed to protect Yayati.

Rama angrily released an arrow at Hanuman who chanted Rama's name continuously. The arrow hit Hanuman's body and broke into two. Rama was surprised to see his arrows disappear after piercing Hanuman's bare chest. *What devotion Hanuman has for me and how determined he is to protect Yayati*, Rama thought. Narada exclaimed to the celestial sages, "See how the Lord's name is more powerful than the Lord himself. Lord Rama's arrows cannot hurt Hanuman because he keeps chanting his name."

236 Hanuman's Matchless Devotion

The fight between Rama and Hanuman was unending. Narad realised that it was time to end this. The power of the Lord's name had been revealed. Narada urged Vishwamitra to rush to Rama and Hanuman and intervene. By now, Rama had fired the Brahmastra which hit Hanuman's chest. Hanuman bared his chest with his hands and Rama was wonderstruck to see his image imprinted in Hanuman's heart as he chanted Rama's name.

Rama was overcome with love and embraced Hanuman. "You have defeated me with your devotion, Hanuman," Rama said. "You have won this battle."

237 Rama's Equal

After the battle between Rama and Hanuman was over, Narada appeared before them with the celestial sages. They now unanimously agreed on the power of Lord Rama's name. "From today, you shall be known as Veer Hanuman," Vishwamitra declared. Yayati accompanied Rama as his guest to Ayodhya. Hanuman returned to Ayodhya and continued serving Rama. "Hanuman, why do you always bow to me and kneel before me when you know that there is no real difference between you and me?"' Rama asked Hanuman one day.

"My Lord, when I am away from you, I know that there is no difference between you and me," Hanuman replied humbly. "But when I appear in front of you, I can approach you only as your slave!"

238 Hanuman's Teaches Shani a Lesson

Once the mischief-maker Shanidev saw Hanuman meditating by a river and decided to tease him. He began pulling at Hanuman's tail. Hanuman warned, "Leave me alone. Don't test my patience!" But Shani kept pestering him. Hanuman lost his patience and wrapping his tail around Shani's body, he swung it up and down, and dashed him against the huge rocks, even as he continued meditating. Soon, a severely injured Shani lost consciousness. When Shani regained consciousness, he apologised for disturbing Hanuman.

"Never disturb me and my devotees," Hanuman warned Shani and gave him oil for his bruises. Shani applied the oil on his wounds and was cured. Shani never disturbed Hanuman again.

239 Sita's Gift to Hanuman

Once, Vibheeshan, who had been crowned the king of Lanka after Ravana's death, paid a visit to Ayodhya. He brought many gifts for everyone. Vibheeshan presented a wonderful necklace made of precious gems to Sita.

"This is a lovely gift, Lord Vibheeshan," Sita exclaimed. "In fact, this necklace is so lovely that I wish to gift it to someone very dear to me. I hope you don't mind."

"Not at all," a pleased Vibheeshan said. "Only you can think of giving away things you like to your near and dear ones."

"Whom shall you give this precious necklace to, dear Sita?" Rama enquired with a smile.

"My Lord, I shall give it to Hanuman," Sita replied. "He has done so much for all of us and yet he has received nothing in return."

"That's an excellent choice," Rama agreed. Even Vibheeshan was happy with Sita's choice as he held Hanuman in very high regard.

Sita gave Hanuman the necklace with the precious gems.

"Here's a gift for you, Hanuman!" she said. Hanuman accepted Sita's gift with humility and thanked her.

240 Hanuman Destroys Sita's Gift

After Hanuman had accepted the precious necklace from Sita, he started inspecting it carefully. He rolled over each and every gem in the necklace many times. Hanuman started removing the gems from the necklace one by one. The people in Rama's court were watching in a puzzled manner. Then, Hanuman put each and every gem near his ear as if to hear something. He scratched his head in confusion and cracked the gems with his teeth till they broke. Then, Hanuman examined the broken pieces of the gems carefully.

"What is Hanuman doing?" one of Rama's ministers exclaimed. Everyone was shocked at this strange behaviour when a disappointed Hanuman threw aside the broken gems.

"Why has Hanuman destroyed the precious necklace gifted to him so lovingly by Sita?" people whispered. Vibheeshan and Sita looked crestfallen as the precious necklace was now reduced to broken pieces and lay scattered on the palace floor. What was particularly strange to everyone was that Hanuman was reknowned for his knowledge, wisdom and intelligence. So what had prompted him to indulge in such reckless behaviour?

241 A Minister Challenges Hanuman

Everyone in Rama's court including Vibheeshan and Sita was outraged when Hanuman destroyed Sita's expensive gift. They asked, "Why did you destroy the necklace? It was a gift from Queen Sita." Hanuman replied, "I am blessed to have received this gift from Sita Mata. But when I did not find Lord Rama's name in the gems of the necklace, I realised it was useless and so I threw it away."

Rama was smiling now, but the people in the court did not understand the logic behind Hanuman's actions. "What about your body?" A minister challenged Hanuman. "Does it have Lord Rama's name on it? Will you throw that away too?"

242 Hanuman Proves His Devotion

Rama's minister was very angry with Hanuman for having destroyed Sita's necklace. He shouted angrily, "You claim that you do not wear anything that does not have Lord Rama's name on it. In that case, you should give up your body as well. Does it have Lord Rama's name written on it?"

Hanuman plucked a hair from his arm and held it next to the surprised minister's ear. The minister heard the sound of 'Rama! Rama! Rama!' pulsating from the hair. He was awestruck and prostrated himself at Hanuman's feet, begging for forgiveness. "I have doubted your devotion towards Lord Rama without understanding your greatness," he said tearfully.

Hanuman embraced the minister lovingly. Rama walked towards Hanuman and embraced him as everyone in the court smiled, including Sita and Vibheeshan.

243 Hanuman and Sita's Sindoor

Once, when Sita was about to enter Rama's bedroom, Hanuman unknowingly followed her. Sita hesitated when he tried to come inside, but couldn't tell him not to. She treated him like her own son. Rama gently addressed him, "Hanuman, you cannot enter this room."

"Why can't I enter this room if Sita Mata can?" Hanuman asked innocently.

"Sita can enter the bedroom because she has sindoor on her forehead. Only a wife who has sindoor on her forehead can enter her husband's bedroom and no one else," Rama explained. Hanuman came outside and pondered. So, sindoor is the qualification that is needed to enter Lord Rama's bedroom. Hanuman had no idea about the ways and practices of human beings as firstly, he was a bachelor and secondly, because these were not practiced in the monkey kingdom.

244 The Significance of Sindoor

Hanuman's curiosity about sindoor was aroused as he realised he didn't know anything about this strange substance. The next day, when he saw Sita smearing the parting of her hair with sindoor, he asked her why she was doing so. Sita replied, "I am applying sindoor to increase Lord Rama's life span."

This sindoor is powerful. It will give Rama a long life, Hanuman thought and rushed outside the palace. He finally found a shop where sindoor was being sold.

245 Hanuman Finds Sindoor

Hanuman demanded a lot of sindoor from the shopkeeper. Reaching the godown, Hanuman emptied the sacks of sindoor all over his body. Then he rolled in the heap of red powder that had fallen on the ground to be totally covered in reddish orange. As Hanuman walked back to the palace, people jeered at him.But Hanuman didn't mind them as he happily approached Rama's palace.

246 Bajrang Bali

Like everyone else, Sita and Rama too were amused when they saw Hanuman entering the court fully smeared with sindoor. Hanuman said with folded hands, "I have heard from Sita Mata that sindoor increases your life span. Smearing my entire body with sindoor will surely make you immortal." Rama descended from his throne and embraced Hanuman lovingly.

"I am amazed by your pure love and devotion towards me, Hanuman," Rama exclaimed in wonder. "You are my greatest devotee. From today, you will also be known as Bajrang Bali." (Bajrang meaning saffron coloured).

247 Rama's Greatest Devotee

Rama turned to his courtiers after embracing Hanuman, "Hanuman is guided by pure devotion and does not care about being ridiculed. That is why Hanuman is my greatest devotee. From today, whoever offers oil and sindoor to Hanuman will have my blessings and all their wishes shall be fulfilled."

"Jai Bajrangbali!" the people at Rama's court chanted loudly. Even today, Hanuman is worshipped with oil and vermilion by his numerous devotees. Hanuman has become a symbol of devotion, loyalty, bravery and wisdom.

248 The Swayambhu Ling

Rama had to perform a special prayer before a Swayambhu Shivling to atone for the sin of killing Ravana, a brahmin. Hanuman was sent to Kashi to fetch it. But he was totally confused as he saw many lings there. He prayed to Lord Rama for help.

Lord Vishnu decided to help him. In fact, it was Lord Vishnu who had gifted Hanuman the mace known as Hanuman Gada which epitomised power and supremacy.

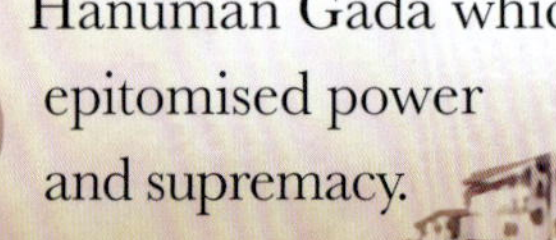

249 Lord Vishnu's Help

Lord Vishnu decided to help Hanuman identify the Swayambhu lingam. He summoned his mount, Garuda and told him to fly to Kasi and help Hanuman identify the Swayambhu Ling.

Garuda immediately rushed to Kasi. Hanuman saw Garuda repeatedly circling around one particular lingam.At the same time, a lizard also made clicking noises near the lingam. Hanuman thanked Garuda and the lizard. He removed the Swayambhu ling and holding it respectfully in one hand, he leaped towards Ayodhya. Bhairava, the guard appointed by the gods to protect Kasi spotted Hanuman flying away with the Swayambhu ling and tried to stop him.

250 Bhairava Attacks Hanuman

Bhairava was furious when he saw Hanuman with the Swayambhu ling. He attacked Hanuman and soon a fierce fight broke out. Both the warriors were evenly matched and the battle raged on till the entire world faced destruction. The gods decided to intervene.

They requested Bhairava, "Please allow Hanuman to take the lingam to Ayodhya. Lord Rama needs to perform a special prayer."

"I agree on one condition," Bhairava stated. "The lizard and Garuda shall be punished for helping Hanuman."

Since then, Garuda does not fly within 45 miles of Kasi and lizards are always mute there.

251 The Jealous Narada

Sage Tumburu was an exceptional veena player. Lord Vishnu was mesmerised when he heard Sage Tumburu's recital. Narada was very jealous when he heard Lord Vishnu showering Tumburu with praise. He thought, *Lord Vishnu never praises me when I play the veena before him. He always praises Tumburu.* Narada decided to teach Tumburu a lesson and started practicing the veena very seriously. He practiced day and night till he thought he had achieved perfection. Narada thought, *I am ready to challenge Tumburu and show him and all the devas that I am the master when it comes to playing the veena*!

252 Indra's Suggestion

Narada went to Indra's court and challenged Tumburu to determine who the better veena player was. The devas present were mesmerised by both their performances.

"That's not enough," Narada said. "You have to judge who the better player is." Indra was in a predicament. He did not want to offend either of the sages. He said to Narada, "I'm afraid that I'm not qualified to judge you. Besides, I might be biased in my judgement as Sage Tumburu plays at my court."

Narada was pleased, yet perplexed. "You speak wisely, Lord Indra," he replied. "But what shall we do?"

"Why don't you approach Lord Vishnu to judge you?" Indra suggested. "He has excellent taste in music after all."

"That's a wonderful idea," Narada exclaimed. "What do you say Tumburu?" Tumburu agreed instantly.

253 Hanuman Judges the Veena Recital

Narada and Tumburu approached Lord Vishnu and played before him. Vishnu was unable to arrive at a decision. He suggested, "Hanuman is one of the best veena players I have heard. He might also have a neutral view." The two went to Hanuman. Hanuman agreed to judge the contest between the two sages in Indra's court. The devas, apsaras and gandharvas gathered to witness the competition. Both the sages played exceptionally well, and Hanuman was at his wit's end as to how to choose the winner. *It's impossible to choose a winner between Sage Narada and Sage Tumburu,* Hanuman thought.

254 Hanuman Finds a Solution

After the two sages had finished playing, Hanuman sat with his eyes closed, praying to Rama to help him with this unique problem. Suddenly, he knew what to do. "Both the sages have played exceptional music," he said. "But they must be put to another test to determine the better veena player." Narada and Tumburu stared at Hanuman. Hanuman held the veena and took out its frets. "Now play it!" he said to Narada and Tumburu. "Can you play the veena without the frets?" a furious Narada challenged. Hanuman took a bamboo stick and slided it on the veena and started playing.

255 Hanuman Plays the Veena

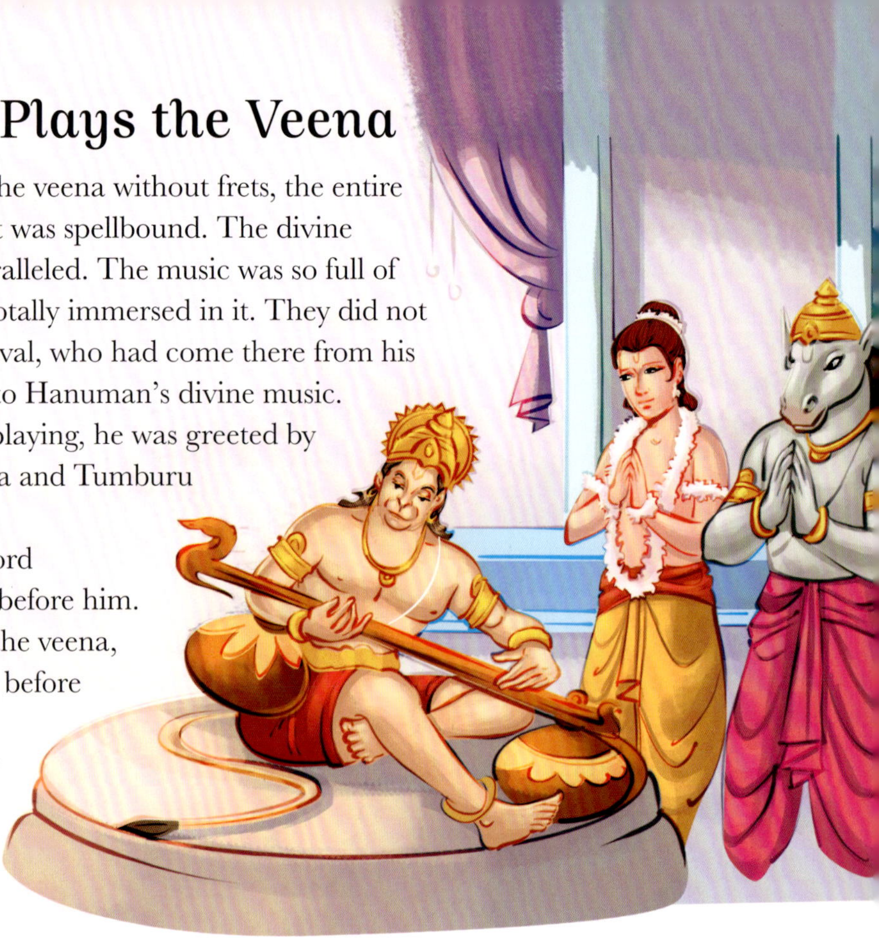

As Hanuman started playing the veena without frets, the entire audience in Lord Indra's court was spellbound. The divine and soulful melody was unparalleled. The music was so full of devotion that everybody was totally immersed in it. They did not even notice Lord Vishnu's arrival, who had come there from his abode in Vaikuntha attracted to Hanuman's divine music. After Hanuman had finished playing, he was greeted by a thunderous applause. Narada and Tumburu accepted defeat

Then, everyone noticed Lord Vishnu's presence and bowed before him. "Truly, you are the master of the veena, Hanuman," they said, bowing before him. Lord Vishnu explained, "Hanuman's music is superior because it is filled with devotion and does not have any ego in it. Hanuman has proved the glory of total surrender to the divine!"

256 Hanuman Fights Lord Ganesha

The mischievous demon Gajasur was upset with Lord Ganesha and decided to teach him a lesson. He approached Hanuman who was chanting Lord Rama's name."Someone is speaking ill about Lord Rama," Gajasur said to Hanuman. Predictably, Hanuman was provoked and demanded to know who had dared to do so.When Gajasur hesitated, Hanuman grabbed his neck angrily.

"He is Ganesha, the son of Lord Shiva," Gajasur cried. Hanuman flew to Ganesha's abode. A fierce battle began between Hanuman and Ganesha. The news of their battle reached Lord Shiva who arrived to stop the fight. Soon Hanuman became aware about Gajasur's trick. He apologised to Lord Ganesha. Lord Ganesha reformed Gajasur and made him his vahana or mount.

257 Hanuman Helps Lord Vishnu

The first time Hanuman assumed his Panchmukhi form or the form with five faces was when he killed Mahiravan. The second time he assumed this form was to help Lord Vishnu. Lord Vishnu was troubled when a demon stole his most powerful weapon, the Sudarshan Chakra. Hanuman offered his services to Lord Vishnu to retrieve the stolen weapon. Lord Vishnu was pleased as the demon was a master in changing his forms and had fled to the depths of the Earth with the Sudarshan Chakra where he would be difficult to find. "May you be victorious," Lord Vishnu blessed Hanuman and gave him the divine weapons needed to defeat the demon. Hanuman assumed his Panchmukhi form with the five faces of Garuda, Narasimha, Hayagreeva, Varaha and Hanuman. This increased his power five times and he killed the demon to retrieve Lord Vishnu's Sudarshan Chakra.

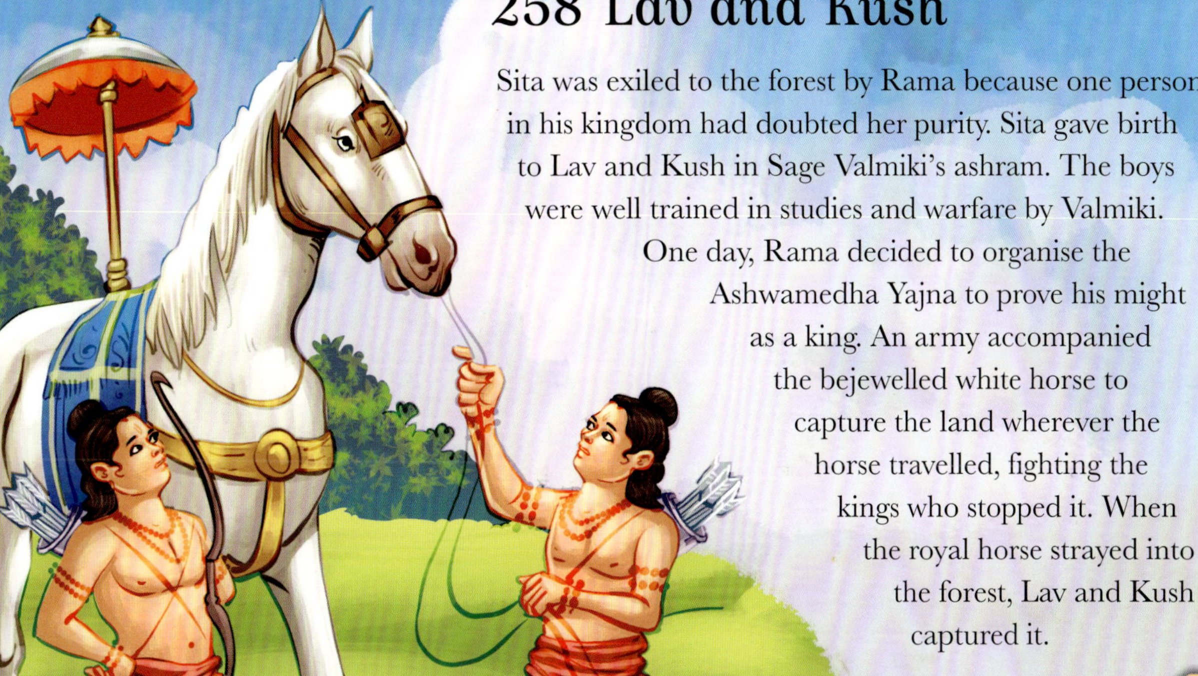

258 Lav and Kush

Sita was exiled to the forest by Rama because one person in his kingdom had doubted her purity. Sita gave birth to Lav and Kush in Sage Valmiki's ashram. The boys were well trained in studies and warfare by Valmiki. One day, Rama decided to organise the Ashwamedha Yajna to prove his might as a king. An army accompanied the bejewelled white horse to capture the land wherever the horse travelled, fighting the kings who stopped it. When the royal horse strayed into the forest, Lav and Kush captured it.

259 Luv and Kush Fight Rama's Army

Sita's sons Lav and Kush captured the Ashwamedha horse of Rama's army. Shatrughna who was accompanied by Hanuman and other warriors requested them to release the horse.

"We will not let your army conquer the land of our ashram," Sita's twin sons replied. They also refused to listen to Hanuman's plea regarding the same. "Release the horse or else you will have to fight us," Shatrughna ordered angrily. "We are ready to fight your army," Lav and Kush declared as they armed themselves with their bows and arrows. *These two are no ordinary boys*, Hanuman thought. An angry Shatrughna ordered his soldiers to untie the horse. But Lav and Kush shot their arrows and injured the soldiers. When more soldiers attacked Lav and Kush, Lav released a weapon that put them all to sleep.

260 Hanuman Fights Rama's Sons

Shatrughna was angry when his two warriors Kalanemi and Pushkal were also defeated by the two boys. Now Shatrughna ordered Hanuman to bring back the Ashwamedha horse. Hanuman uprooted a tree and threw it at the boys. Lav's arrows destroyed the tree into pieces. Hanuman then captured Lav by winding his tail around him. But Kush came to his brother's rescue with a volley of arrows that freed Lav. *I think I know who these boys are*, Hanuman thought suddenly. *No one else is capable of such prowess*! Hanuman's thoughts were interrupted as Lav and Kush shot arrows that bound Hanuman.

"The monkey is our prisoner!" Kush exclaimed in joy. "Let's take him and show him to mother," Lav stated and Kush agreed. *That is what I also want, my dear boys*, Hanuman thought happily.

261 Hanuman Meets Sita

Lav and Kush dragged Hanuman to the ashram."Look mother!" they exclaimed. "We've got a monkey as a prisoner." Sita was shocked to see that her sons had captured Hanuman."Oh, my sons! What have you done?" she exclaimed. Hanuman was weeping tears of joy."I had guessed that these brave boys were sons of my Lord. How fortunate I am!" Hanuman exclaimed. Lav and Kush were puzzled that their mother knew their prisoner. "You have captured the mighty Hanuman. Release him at once!" Sita ordered her sons, who obeyed and freed Hanuman. Just then, Valmiki arrived and Hanuman bowed before him. As Hanuman was set free, Valmiki requested him to keep the identity of Lav and Kush a secret. "It's not yet time for people to know about Rama's sons," he explained. "As you command," Hanuman replied, and requested permission to visit the ashram, which was granted by Valmiki.

262 Hanuman's Appetite

Hanuman now often visited the ashram to meet Sita. He was fond of eating the simple food prepared by Sita. One day, he was feeling particularly hungry. As Sita served him the food, he kept on eating. Soon, all the food in Sita's kitchen was finished, and Hanuman's appetite was still not satisfied. In desperation, Sita prayed to Rama as it was a dishonour for a guest to go hungry. Rama appeared in Sita's prayers and asked her to serve a leaf of Tulsi along with a morsel of food to Hanuman. Sita did as instructed, and Hanuman felt full at once.

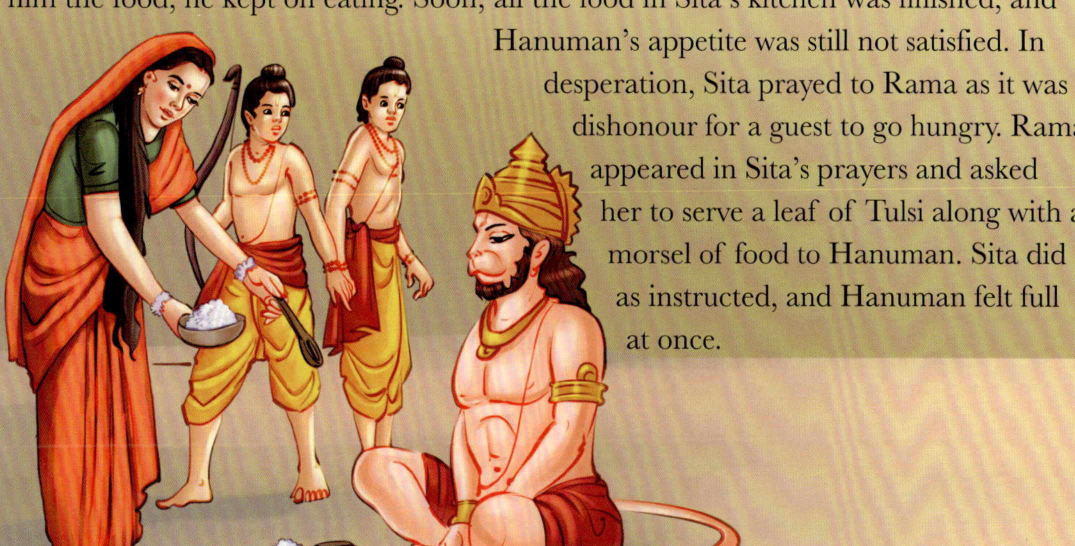

263 Rama's Army in Devpur

After conquering many lands, the horse and the army of Rama's Ashwamedha Yajna reached Devpur which was ruled by King Veermani. When the Ashwamedha horse galloped into Devpur, Veermani's son Rukmangad intercepted it. This meant a declaration of war between the armies of Devpur and Ayodhya. When King Veermani heard about the incident, he summoned his son."Lord Rama is our friend. Return the horse to his army at once."

264 Hanuman's Advice

When King Veermani asked his son Rukmangad to release Rama's Ashwamedha horse, he refused. Veermani agreed reluctantly to continue the fight. Meanwhile, Hanuman informed Shatrughna that Lord Shiva had promised his devotee Veermani that he himself shall always protect Devpur. "We might have to face Lord Shiva in battle," Hanuman warned Shatrughna and advised, "We should hold talks with King Veermani. If he doesn't understand even then, we should inform Lord Rama and seek his advice. It is foolhardy to battle with Lord Shiva." But Bharat's son Pushkal was eager to fight. So Shatrughna declared, "We will fight."

265 Shatrughna's Army Wins

Shatrughna ignored Hanuman's advice and decided to fight to reclaim the Ashwamedha horse. The war between the two armies began. After a fierce duel, Veermani fainted in his chariot under the onslaught of Pushkal's arrows. His brother Veersahi tried all his divine weapons on Hanuman but failed to cause him any harm. Finally, Hanuman uprooted a huge tree and flung it at Veersahi's chariot, breaking it into pieces and injuring Veersahi, who lost consciousness. Veermani regained consciousness that very moment. Seeing his army defeated, he desperately prayed to Lord Shiva for help.

266 Shiva's Army Attacks

Realising that Devpur was in trouble, Lord Shiva summoned his trusted aide Veerabhadra to help Veermani. Under Veerabhadra's leadership, Lord Shiva's army of ganas including Nandi and Bhringi arrived to defend Devpur. Shatrughna's army shivered in fright when they saw the fearsome army approach. Bharat's son Pushkal offered to fight Veerabhadra who was equal to Lord Shiva in prowess. Hanuman fought with Nandi as Shatrughna faced Bhringi. But Pushkal was no match in battle against the mighty Veerabhadra and was soon killed. Shatrughna too was bound by Bhringi's powerful weapon. The terrible battle between Hanuman and Nandi was unending and threatened to destroy the entire world.

267 Lord Shiva Steps In

Hanuman was enraged when he saw that Pushkal had been killed and Shatrughna was bound. He immediately freed Shatrughna and started fighting so valiantly that no one from Lord Shiva's army could match him. Lord Shiva himself was forced to come to the battlefield to fight. Soon, Shatrughna was knocked down senseless by Lord Shiva's trident. *I now have no option but to fight Mahadeva,* Hanuman thought. "My Lord," Hanuman bowed before Lord Shiva. "I am compelled to fight with you against my wishes," he said humbly. Lord Shiva stated, "I am forced to fight Rama's army as I have sworn to protect Devpur and my devotee Veermani."

268 Hanuman Pleases Lord Shiva

Reluctantly, Hanuman and Lord Shiva were forced to fight each other. Lord Shiva released his trident when Hanuman charged at him with his mace. Hanuman cut the trident into pieces and an angry Shiva then released a powerful weapon at Hanuman. But he was surprised when Hanuman dodged this weapon and attacked Lord Shiva with a volley of trees, boulders and rocks.

"You have pleased me with your bravery, Hanuman," Lord Shiva finally said. "Ask for any boon except for victory in this battle." "My Lord, please grant a ceasefire. Also bless me to revive Shatrughna and bring back Pushkal to life by fetching the Sanjeevani plant from the Himalayas," Hanuman requested. "But Pushkal has died a warrior's death," Lord Shiva smiled. "You should be proud of him. Why do you want to bring him back to life?"

269 Hanuman Saves Pushkal

Hanuman bowed before Lord Shiva and said, "Lord Rama sent me with the army for a purpose. How will I show him my face now, with Pushkal killed and Shatrughna unconscious? I'd rather give up my life trying to protect them."

Lord Shiva said, "You are truly the greatest devotee of Lord Rama. Go to the Himalayas. Revive Shatrughna and bring back Pushkal to life. The battle will begin only after your return." Hanuman flew to the Drongiri Mountain. He returned with the herb and brought back the dead Pushkal to life and revived Shatrughna. As the two armies got ready to face each other again, Hanuman advised Shatrughna, "We cannot defeat Lord Shiva in battle. Let us pray to Lord Rama to help us!"

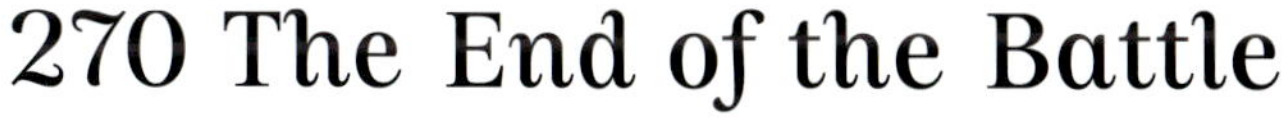

270 The End of the Battle

After praying to Lord Rama, Hanuman went to fight Lord Shiva. He was the only one who could fight him in Shatrughna's army. After a fierce battle, Shiva knocked him unconsciousness. Lord Rama himself appeared on the battlefield and revived him. Then, Rama bowed before Lord Shiva who immediately lay down his weapons, and advised Veermani to do the same.

Rama addressed Lord Shiva, "I defeated Ravana with your blessings. This Ashwamedha Yajna is also taking place with your grace. Please forgive my army and put an end to this foolish battle."

Shiva then told Rama that he was forced to fight to protect his devotee Veermani and that he had already advised him to return the Ashwamedha horse.

271 Hanuman's Wisdom

After the battle ended, Veermani apologised to Rama. "The horse was caught mistakenly by my son. Please forgive him as we had no option but to fight as true Kshatriyas," he said, returning the Ashwamedha horse.

Upon Rama's invitation, after the Ashwamedha ceremony, Lord Shiva arrived in Ayodhya, where Rama welcomed him with great warmth. Rama ordered Hanuman to serve some fresh milk to Shiva. Hanuman handed the pot of milk to Rama instead. Hanuman explained, "As I'm your mere servant, it will be a dishonour if I serve Lord Shiva the milk. You should serve him." Rama smiled at Hanuman's humility and Shiva embraced him. "Hanuman, you will always be blessed because of your wisdom and devotion to Lord Rama," he said.

272 Narada's Curiosity

Once, Narada arrived playing his Veena to meet Rama in Ayodhya. He saw Hanuman guarding Rama's palace. "Narayana Narayana!" Narada exclaimed. "How are you, Hanuman?" "Greetings, O holy one," Hanuman bowed before him. Then Narada entered the palace where he saw Rama writing something. "Why are you doing such boring work which you can delegate to someone else?" he asked. Rama replied that the work could not be entrusted to anyone else. Narada could not control his curiosity now. "Please tell me what you are writing down, My Lord," he pleaded.

"What will you do by knowing?" Rama smiled and replied. Narada could not control his curiosity now. "Please tell me what you are writing down, My Lord," he pleaded again.

273 Rama's List of Devotees

Narada was curious to know what Rama was writing down. "Every day, I write down the names of all the devotees who pray to me," Rama revealed. "It makes it easier for me to remember them." Narada then asked eagerly, "Can you please tell me where my name is on the list?" Rama invited him to take a look. Narada was elated to see his name on top of the list. *Why isn't Hanuman's name on Lord Rama's list of devotees?* Narada thought. *He is a special devotee of Lord Rama. How could Lord Rama have forgotten to put Hanuman's name on this special list?*

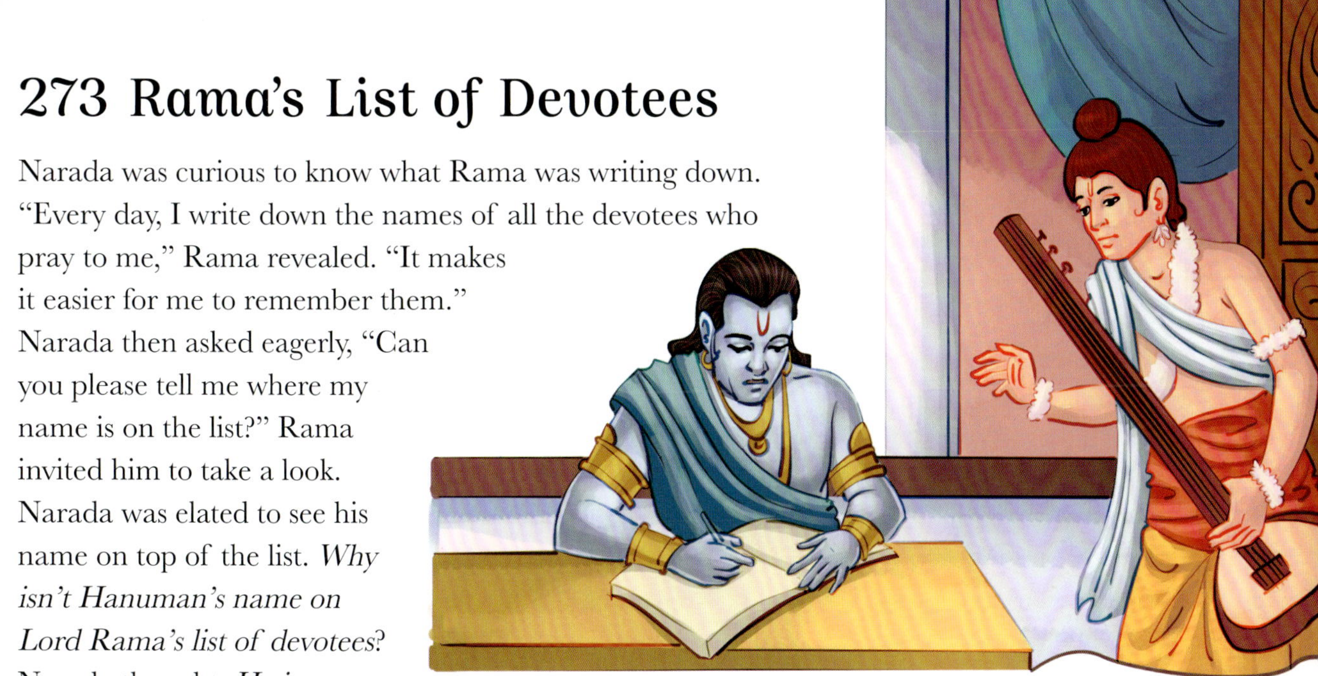

"I have some bad news for you ," he told Hanuman while leaving the palace. "Lord Rama was writing down the names of his devotees and your name is nowhere there!"

274 Rama's Second List of Devotees

Hanuman was surprised when Narada informed him that his name was missing from Rama's list of devotees. "Maybe Lord Rama does not think me capable enough to write down my name in his book," a disappointed Hanuman said. "But I have also noticed that he has a smaller book in which he writes." Narada was curious now to find out about this smaller book. He entered Rama's chambers again and demanded to see the smaller list.

"There are some devotees of mine whose devotion is so supreme that I have to worship them too," Rama explained as he handed his smaller book to Narada. Narada saw that Hanuman's name was on top of this list!

275 Hanumad Ramayana

Hanuman wrote his version of the Ramayana on the peaks of the Himalayas by using his nails. One day, Sage Valmiki heard about Hanuman's version of the Ramayana or the Hanumad Ramayana and decided to read it. He travelled to the Himalayas where Hanuman was busy writing on a mountain wall. Hanuman was delighted to see the sage. "I have written my version of the Ramayana on these mountain walls. You will be the best person to tell me if I have missed anything out. May I request you to read my version?"

Valmiki was eager to read Hanuman's version of the Ramayana to see if he himself had missed out something. He patiently read what Hanuman had so painstakingly written on the walls. The body of work was a massive one and it took Valmiki a few years to finish reading the Hanumad Ramayana.

276 Hanuman Destroys His Work

When Valmiki finished reading the Hanumad Ramayana, he was moved by the sheer brilliance of the work. *How wonderfully Hanuman has written down everything*, Valmiki thought. *My own version of the Ramayana pales in comparison.* Valmiki's disappointment showed on his face and was noticed by Hanuman.

"Why do you look so disappointed?" Hanuman asked.

Valmiki replied, "I have also prepared an account of the Ramayana with great effort. But that would never match the beauty of your creation and will definitely be overlooked and ignored. But I have no regrets about it as your work is not only original but much better."

Hanuman was thoughtful for a while. Then, Hanuman did something that totally shocked Valmiki. Hanuman uprooted the entire mountain that contained the Hanumad Ramayana. He flew with the mountain to the ocean and dropped the mountain there, which sank to the very depths.

277 Valmiki's Vow

Hanuman threw the mountain containing the Hanumad Ramayana into the ocean. He explained to Valmiki, "Your greatness makes you think that my work is superior to yours. It would hurt me if people do not remember your great work because of my simple effort." Moved by Hanuman's sacrifice Valmiki vowed to take rebirth just to sing Hanuman's richly deserved praises. Many years later, a huge rock was discovered floating in the ocean. The great poet Kalidas identified it as the Hanumad Ramayana and glorified Hanuman's character in his version of the Ramayana.

278 Hanuman Goes to Satsang

Rama asked Hanuman why he did not go and listen to the religious talks of the sages. "You keep serving me," Rama said. "But you should listen to the kathas of the sages about God." "I wonder how useful it will be for me to listen to the sages talk about God when I have found God in your service," Hanuman replied. "It will increase your devotion if you listen to the sermon of a holy sage," Rama explained. "Whom do you suggest I go to, My Lord?" Hanuman asked. "Shri Kag Bhushundi is a sage of the highest order," Rama replied. "You should go and hear him speak. He sits on the Nilgiri mountains and recites his sermons daily. Even the Devas go and listen to him."

Hanuman reached the Nilgiri Mountains and joined the devotees in the satsang listening to the sage. But he was surprised as his topic for the day was Hanuman himself. The sage spoke about Hanuman's heroics. But Hanuman was stunned as the heroics mentioned by the sage had not been performed by him.

279 Hanuman's Confusion

Hanuman finished attending the satsang and returned to Rama's palace. "What was the topic for today?" Rama asked. "The topic was 'Crossing of the Ocean' and 'The Burning of Lanka'," an embarrassed Hanuman replied. "But I think the sage exaggerated my exploits greatly." "Shri Kag Bhushundi is not an ordinary sage, Hanuman," he replied. "You should not doubt his words." "I did not do the things the sage mentioned," Hanuman replied. "He said that Hanuman reached Lanka on one foot and burnt Lanka with flames that emerged from his mouth." Suddenly, Rama took out his ring and dropped it."Oh, Hanuman!" he exclaimed. "I dropped my ring. Please get it for me." Hanuman tried to pick up the ring but it slid away. As the ring rolled away, Hanuman ran after it. After a long chase, the ring entered a huge cave in the Sumeru Mountains. Hanuman tried to enter the cave but found his path blocked by a huge monkey.

"Stop!" the monkey ordered Hanuman. "I am the gatekeeper of this cave and you cannot enter without my permission."

280 Two Hanumans

"I'm Hanuman, the servant of Lord Rama!" Hanuman introduced himself. The huge monkey laughed, "The real Hanuman is sitting inside this cave meditating." Thinking it to be a Leela of Lord Rama, Hanuman requested him that he wanted to pay his respects to Lord Hanuman. When the meditating monkey heard this, he asked him to be escorted inside with respect. As Hanuman entered the cave, his eyes were dazzled by the light that emerged from the huge monkey. The cave glittered with the light from his body.

281 The Lord's Power

"Welcome, Hanuman," the powerful monkey greeted Hanuman."Who are you?" a surprised Hanuman asked.

"I am Hanuman too," the monkey replied. "The katha you heard from Shri Kag Bhushundi is from another time and another Universe. You assumed he was speaking about you, but he wasn't. In fact, you are talking to the Hanuman he was talking about." "This is unbelievable," Hanuman exclaimed.

"But it's also true," the monkey replied. "In every Universe, the Lord keeps taking incarnations to abolish evil. It is He who grants his devotees the special powers they possess to destroy evil. I am the Hanuman who travelled to Lanka on one foot and burned it with the flames from my mouth. The only difference is that while you used your tail, I used my mouth! But remember that this power is not yours or mine. It is actually the Lord's power!" "It is such an honour to meet you," Hanuman bowed respectfully before his namesake. The second Hanuman rose and embraced Hanuman warmly. "The feeling is mutual, my dear Hanuman!" he exclaimed.

282 Rama Consoles Hanuman

After Sita returned to Mother Earth, Hanuman was very sad. He sat meditating in a corner with his eyes closed, disinterested in anything else. Tears flowed from his eyes when he realised that his beloved Sita Mata had left the world. Rama approached Hanuman worriedly.

"Don't be sad, Hanuman," Rama stated. "All of us who are born have to die. But you shall be glad to know that Sita and I will be reunited soon after I leave this world."

Hanuman was very sad to learn that Lord Rama would also be leaving him one day like Sita Mata. "I regret that I couldn't give you anything in return for your love and devotion, Hanuman," Rama apologised. "Would you like to accompany me to Vaikuntha after this life?" A surprised Hanuman asked,"But will you be there as Lord Rama in Vaikuntha? That is Lord Vishnu's abode."

Rama smiled and replied, "Yes, but I shall be there not as Rama, but as Lord Mahavishnu. You see, Lord Vishnu is the cause, and Lord Rama is the effect."

283 Yama Fails to Take Rama

When Rama offered Hanuman a place in Vaikuntha, Hanuman was thoughtful. He did not want to live anywhere without Rama. He decided to stay back in Ayodhya and continue meditating on Rama. Pleased with Hanuman's devotion, Rama granted him the boon of immortality. Thus, Hanuman is one of the seven Chiranjeevis or immortals on Earth. When the Earth had been finally rid of all evil and peace prevailed, Rama prepared to go back to devlok. Yamraj, the god of death came to take Rama but could not. Yamraj was summoned by Lord Brahma. "Why hasn't Lord Rama quit his mortal abode yet?" Lord Brahma demanded. "I have tried to get Lord Rama from Earth many times," Yamraj explained. "But Hanuman guards him so well that I have been unable to breach his defences and take Rama's life."

284 Hanuman in Pataal

Yamraj expressed his helplessness in ending Lord Rama's life span on Earth. Lord Brahma explained to Rama, "We must trick Hanuman in some manner so that you can be released from Earth." Rama devised a plan to keep Hanuman busy. One day, he dropped his ring on the floor. It slipped into a crack in the floor and disappeared. "I shall fetch it for you, My Lord," Hanuman volunteered. He reduced his form and entered the crack. To his surprise, the crack formed an endless tunnel. After a long time, Hanuman discovered that he had arrived in Pataal Lok.

285 Hanuman Meets Vasuki

Hanuman was searching for Rama's ring when he was greeted by the Snake King Vasuki, who was aware of Rama's plan and had agreed to help him. Vasuki asked Hanuman to follow him to a cave which was dazzling with many golden rings. "These are all Lord Rama's rings. Take any one." Seeing Hanuman's bewildered look, he explained, "An incarnation of Lord Rama arrives on Earth whenever evil prevails, and then departs. This incarnation should leave now. But you are not allowing him to go!" Vasuki then explained Vishnu's incarnations on Earth in detail to Hanuman, who understood everything now.

286 The Birth of Krishna

Hanuman was deeply saddened that it was time for Lord Rama to depart. Rama said, "We shall be reunited in my next incarnation in the Dwapar Yuga as Krishna." Hanuman said that he would eagerly wait for that day.

Rama and Lakshmana ended their avatars on Earth by entering the Sarayu River, and Hanuman left to engage in deep penance in the Himalayas. Hanuman was informed of Lord Krishna's impending birth towards the end of Dwapar Yuga. The prospect of being reunited with his Lord again elated Hanuman. His help was crucial to any incarnation of Lord Vishnu on Earth and that is why he had been granted the boon of immortality.

287 Narada Meets Hanuman

Narada was deputed by the gods to unite Hanuman and Lord Krishna. He travelled to the Himalayas where Hanuman was meditating. Narad informed him about Krishna's exploits and urged him to go to Dwarka and meet Lord Krishna. Hanuman protested, "I am a mere servant of the Lord. I do not wish to insult him by going to see him before he orders me to present myself before him." Narada had no reply to counter Hanuman's strong logic. He thought, *If you do not visit the Lord, I shall ensure that the Lord visits you Himself.*

288 Narada Meets Krishna

Narada visited Dwarka and told Krishna, "I urged Hanuman to meet you, but he said that he is just a humble servant and it would be improper for him to visit his Lord without being summoned. He shall wait till you decide to see him." Krishna replied that Hanuman was his truest devotee and he would fulfil his wish.

Krishna and Narada decided to visit Hanuman on Ram Navami, Lord Rama's birthday.

Narada suggested that Krishna should meet Hanuman as Lord Rama. "Why is that?" Krishna enquired with a smile."Hanuman is devoted to Lord Rama and may not recognise you in the form of Krishna," Narada explained.

Krishna agreed.

289 Rama Navami

Disguised as brahmins, Krishna and Narada arrived at a small village temple where Hanuman was performing a puja on Rama's birthday, disguised as a priest. The two of them sat among the worshippers. Soon, Hanuman finished his prayers and started distributing the prasad to the devotees. Krishna was seated right beside Narada. As soon as Hanuman served them food, his eyes fell on Krishna's feet. He forgot about serving the food and was transfixed, staring at him. "Serve us the food!" Krishna said with a smile. "I am hungry!" Hanuman instantly recognised him and fell at his feet. Krishna froze the time around them. Narada and Hanuman were revealed in their original form and Krishna took Lord Rama's form.

290 Narada Taught a Lesson

When Krishna revealed himself in Lord Rama's form, Hanuman was elated. "The Lord has arrived to grant your wish to see him, Hanuman," Narada said. Hanuman replied that the darshan was incomplete until he had paid his respects to Sita Mata. Krishna promised to invite him to Dwarka soon, where he could meet Sita Mata. Krishna referred to Rukmini, who too was an incarnation of Goddess Lakshmi, as Sita. "I shall need your help to eliminate the evil forces from Earth in this Yuga too," Krishna revealed.

"I'm always at your service, My Lord," Hanuman replied. Krishna and Narada then said goodbye to Hanuman. "I was sure Hanuman would recognise me in any form," Krishna said to Narada as they returned. "I assumed Rama's form just to teach you a lesson."

291 Krishna's Plan

Krishna decided to grant Hanuman the Rama-Sita darshan. With his divine vision he saw that Hanuman was in Kubera's garden. He ordered Garuda to fetch some divine lotus flowers from Kubera's garden. Hanuman saw Garuda plucking the flowers without Kubera's permission, and rebuked him. "I'm taking these flowers for Lord Krishna and do not need anybody's permission." Garuda replied proudly. Hanuman angrily seized Garuda under his arm and flew towards Dwarka.

Meanwhile, Krishna asked Rukmini to take the form of Sita. "Hanuman is coming and he's very angry," Krishna told her. "Only a darshan of Rama-Sita can calm him down or else he will destroy Dwarka and drag it down to the sea."

292 Hanuman's Ram-Sita Darshan

Krishna and Rukmini assumed the forms of Rama and Sita. When Hanuman reached Dwarka, the Sudarshan Chakra stopped his way. Hanuman grabbed it and put it under his other armpit. Krishna and Rukmini welcomed him. Overjoyed to see the divine couple, he exclaimed, "My darshan is finally complete!"

"What's under your armpits, Hanuman?" Krishna asked. Hanuman told them that he had to hold the bird and the chakra captive since they disturbed him. On Krishna's request, Hanuman released Garuda and the Sudarshan Chakra who flew at a respectable distance away from him. Glaring at the trembling Garuda, Hanuman requested humbly that if the Lord needed lotus flowers, he should directly ask him.

293 Krishna Seeks Hanuman's Help

Despite Krishna's advise to be like Rama - humble despite all glories, Satyabhama, Garuda and Sudarshan Chara remained full of false pride. "You had been born as Lord Rama," Satyabhama said to Krishna. "Was Sita as beautiful as me?" Garuda asked him, "My Lord, could Lord Rama's devotee Hanuman fly as fast as me?" Sudarshan Chakra boasted, "If Rama had a weapon like me, he would have achieved greater glories!"

I must teach all three of them a lesson they will never forget, Krishna thought. *Only Hanuman can help me.*

294 Garuda Confronts Hanuman

Using his divine powers, Krishna summoned Hanuman to Dwarka and briefed him. Hanuman entered Dwarka's orchard as an ordinary monkey. He started eating the fruits, breaking the twigs and uprooting the trees there. Krishna ordered Garuda to capture that monkey. An overconfident Garuda arrived at the orchard to see the monkey sitting on a tree, eating a mango. Garuda shouted at him to climb down, but the monkey ignored him. Garuda shouted, "I am the king of the birds. How dare you disobey me? Come down at once to meet Lord Krishna."

Hanuman replied, "I'm a devotee of Lord Rama. I'm not interested in meeting your Lord Krishna!"

295 Garuda's Pride Shattered

When the monkey ignored him, a furious Garuda attacked him with his sharp beak and claws. Hanuman coiled his tail around Garuda's body and flew towards the ocean, throwing Garuda into the deep waters. Garuda rushed back to complain to Krishna who told him that the monkey was none other than Hanuman. "I wish I could have asked Hanuman if he can fly faster than me," Garuda exclaimed. "Why don't you fly to Hanuman and ask him to race you back here?" Krishna suggested. "Tell him I'm waiting to see him at Dwarka."

296 Garuda Goes to Fetch Hanuman

Krishna decided to teach Garuda a lesson in humility. When Garuda reached Hanuman, he said, "Krishna wants to meet you. Please come with me." Hanuman replied that he would come after completing some work. "I was hoping we could fly together so I could test your flying speed," Garuda stated.

"Why don't you fly ahead at full speed?" Hanuman suggested. "I shall follow in some time. Let's see if you reach before me." Garuda took up Hanuman's challenge and flew rapidly towards Dwarka.

297 Sudarshan Chakra and Garuda Humbled

When Hanuman reached Krishna's palace, Sudarshan Chakra asked haughtily where he was going. Hanuman was in a hurry and put the Chakra in his mouth and spluttered it out as he fell at Krishna's feet. Sudarshan Chakra's pride was humbled. *Lord Rama did not need a weapon like me as he had the mighty Hanuman with him*, he thought. Garuda arrived just then and was stunned to see Hanuman sitting at Krishna's feet. "I hope you've got your answer about Hanuman's flying speed," Krishna said to Garuda.

298 Hanuman's Role in the Mahabharata War

Hanuman pointed at Satyabhama who was sitting beside Krishna and asked, "Why is this woman dressed like Sita Mata?" Satyabhama's false pride was totally crushed. After destroying the false pride of Garuda, Sudarshan Chakra, and Satyabhama, Krishna revealed to Hanuman the reason for his incarnation on Earth.He told him of the impending Mahabharata war in which Hanuman would have to support the Pandavas. Krishna also revealed, "Bheema is your half-brother. But you cannot take active part in the battle as you have no match in this Yuga. You shall grace the flag on Arjuna's chariot."

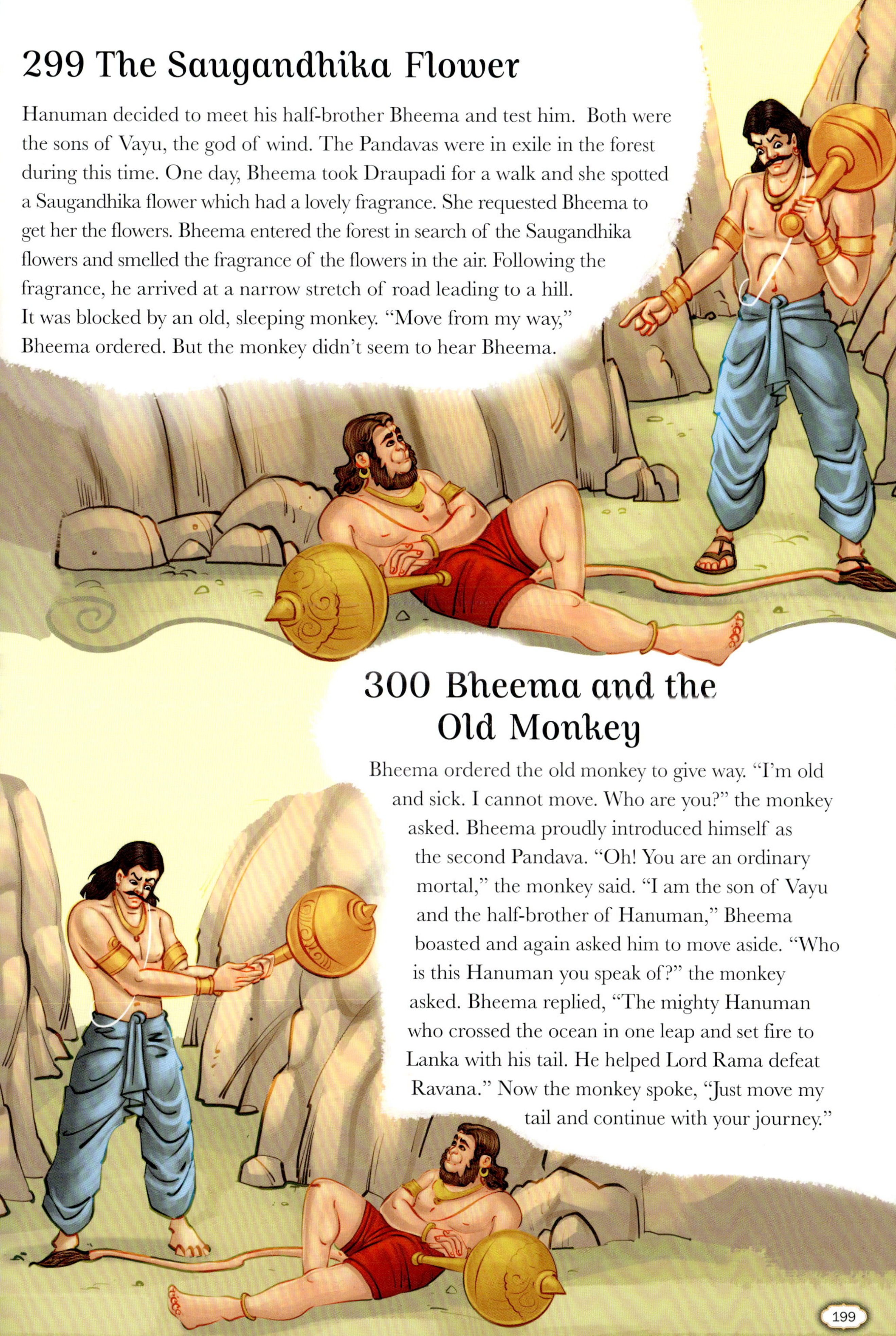

299 The Saugandhika Flower

Hanuman decided to meet his half-brother Bheema and test him. Both were the sons of Vayu, the god of wind. The Pandavas were in exile in the forest during this time. One day, Bheema took Draupadi for a walk and she spotted a Saugandhika flower which had a lovely fragrance. She requested Bheema to get her the flowers. Bheema entered the forest in search of the Saugandhika flowers and smelled the fragrance of the flowers in the air. Following the fragrance, he arrived at a narrow stretch of road leading to a hill. It was blocked by an old, sleeping monkey. "Move from my way," Bheema ordered. But the monkey didn't seem to hear Bheema.

300 Bheema and the Old Monkey

Bheema ordered the old monkey to give way. "I'm old and sick. I cannot move. Who are you?" the monkey asked. Bheema proudly introduced himself as the second Pandava. "Oh! You are an ordinary mortal," the monkey said. "I am the son of Vayu and the half-brother of Hanuman," Bheema boasted and again asked him to move aside. "Who is this Hanuman you speak of?" the monkey asked. Bheema replied, "The mighty Hanuman who crossed the ocean in one leap and set fire to Lanka with his tail. He helped Lord Rama defeat Ravana." Now the monkey spoke, "Just move my tail and continue with your journey."

301 Bheema Humbled

Bheema was getting late. Disdainfully, he tried to move the tail. But to his utter surprise, he couldn't. It seemed that the tail was made of stone. The monkey laughed, "What's taking you so long to lift my tail?" Angrily, Bheema heaved at it again. But it still did not move. The old monkey had crushed Bheema's pride. *He is not an ordinary monkey! He must be a divine form in disguise*, Bheema rightly thought. Hanuman had disguised himself as an old monkey to test Bheema and to teach him a lesson in humility. Bheema accepted defeat and fell at the monkey's feet asking him to reveal his true identity.

302 Hanuman Advises Bheema

When Bheema fell at his feet, Hanuman revealed his true form as Bheema's half-brother and embraced him.Hanuman said to Bheema, "Every battle is won with a combination of brain and brawn. It is also important to be humble and use our strength to protect the oppressed." Bheema thanked Hanuman for his valuable advice and told him he would always abide by it. But he refused his offer to help him win the war. Bheema said with folded hands, "I know it will be child's play for you. But that's something only we have to do."

303 Hanuman's Promise

Hanuman was pleased when Bheema refused his help to destroy the Kauravas. He blessed him, "When you roar at your enemies to challenge them, my roar will join yours to create terror in their hearts. I shall also sit on the flagstaff of Arjuna's chariot during the battle. Emerge victorious in this battle of justice."

My mighty elder brother has taught me patience and humility! Bheema thought gratefully. Hanuman then reminded Bheema that Draupadi must be waiting for the Saugandhika flowers. *He knows about that as well*, an amazed Bheema thought. Then as they embraced, he requested Hanuman to show him the magnificient form he had assumed when he crossed the ocean to fly to Lanka.

304 Hanuman's Magnificient Form

On Bheema's request, Hanuman revealed his magnificient form. The entire area was filled with a divine, blinding light. Bheema had to close his eyes as it was impossible for mortals to face the shine of that light. "Having seen your magnificient form," Bheema said, "Now, I'm confident that I shall defeat all my enemies in battle." Hanuman gave Bheema the directions to the pond of Kubera's garden where the Saugandhika flowers bloomed. Bheema found the pond, defeated Kubera's soldiers single-handedly, and got the Saugandhika flowers for Draupadi.

305 Hanuman's Thread and the Pandavas

Once, Lord Krishna advised Draupadi to worship Hanuman to ward off evil in her life. After worshipping Hanuman, Draupadi wore the holy thread given by the priest around her neck. Arjuna forced her to throw it away. Draupadi took off the thread but kept it safely. Veda Vyasa once visited them and remarked, "If Draupadi had still worn Lord Hanuman's thread, you would have lived peacefully for these thirteen years in the kingdom." Draupadi immediately wore the thread and Yuddishthira and the Pandavas prayed to Hanuman. Soon, Yudhishthira regained his kingdom with Hanuman's blessings.

306 Hanuman Appears Before Arjuna

Arjuna was very proud of his archery skills. He had also heard that Lord Rama was the greatest archer ever. Once he reached Rameshwaram on a spiritual quest and visited the bridge built by the monkeys to transport them to Lanka. *I wonder why the bridge was built with rocks, stones and boulders instead of Lord Rama's arrows if he was the greatest archer*, he wondered. He wanted to meet Hanuman and ask him this question. He prayed to Hanuman devotedly to meet him. Hanuman finally appeared before him.

307 Arjuna's Pride

Arjuna bowed before Hanuman and asked him why Lord Rama had not built the bridge with his arrows instead of using rocks and boulders. Hanuman laughed, "The arrows would not bear the weight of the heavy monkeys and bears in our army. Lord Ram was God himself. Are you questioning his work and ability?" Hanuman asked.

Arjuna boasted, "I can easily build a bridge of arrows strong enough to hold any weight. I can outshine Lord Rama's archery skills." Offended, Hanuman decided to crush Arjuna's pride.

308 Arjuna's Ego Shattered

When Arjuna questioned Lord Rama's competence, Hanuman challenged him to build a bridge of arrows that would withstand his weight. Overconfident, Arjuna vowed to jump into a burning pyre if the bridge built by him broke with Hanuman's weight. Arjuna shot his arrows into the water as Hanuman chanted Lord Rama's name. Soon, a mighty bridge of arrows was ready. As Hanuman uttered Lord Rama's name and placed his tail on it, the entire bridge collapsed. Arjuna's ego was totally shattered.

309 The Witness

Arjuna had lost the bet. To keep his word of honour, he built a wooden pyre and lit it. As he was about to enter it, a brahmin appeared. Arjuna related the details of the bet between him and Hanuman. "Was there a witness to your bet?" the brahmin asked. When Arjuna denied this, the brahmin said, "No bet is valid without a witness. Build the bridge again. I shall be the witness." Arjuna prayed to Krishna and built the bridge again. Hanuman walked and jumped on it, but it did not collapse. Then, Hanuman and Arjuna saw the brahmin supporting the bridge with his shoulders.

310 Devotion Wins

Hanuman and Arjuna realised that the brahmin was no ordinary being. When asked, the brahmin revealed he was Krishna. Hanuman understood that Lord Rama and Lord Krishna were one. Both Arjuna and Hanuman fell at Krishna's feet. Krishna embraced them and said, "As Hanuman took Lord Rama's name, he brought down the bridge. But as Arjuna took my name the second time, Hanuman failed. But in reality, no one failed and only devotion won!"

311 Offerings to Hanuman

There are two legends behind the offerings of betel leaves and butter to Hanuman. Once, Sita met Hanuman in a garden full of betel leaves. Hanuman bowed before Sita who showered a few betel leaves to bless Hanuman. The legend behind the offering of butter to Hanuman has its roots in the battle between Rama and Ravana. Ravana was frustrated when none of his arrows could kill Rama. He began to rain his arrows on Hanuman, who was carrying Rama, and injured him. When they returned to their camp, Rama himself administered cool butter on Hanuman's wounds to heal them. Ever since, devotees offer betel leaves and butter to Hanuman while worshipping him.

312 Hanuman's Roar

When the battle of Kurukshetra began, Hanuman sat on the flagstaff of Arjuna's chariot to protect it. He also joined his roar with Bheema's to challenged the enemies. One day, there was a fierce fight between Arjuna and Karna. As Karna rained arrows on Arjuna, one arrow hit Krishna's protective armour exposing Krishna's body. A furious Hanuman roared so ferociously that Karna's bow fell from his hand. Both the armies fled the battlefield in fear.

313 Hanuman's Rage Scares Karna

When Hanuman roared, even Krishna was alarmed. Hanuman's tail had risen and the fingers of his hands were clenched in anger. His teeth were chattering in rage. Seeing this dangerous form of Hanuman, Karna and his charioteer Shalya shivered in fright. Krishna spoke angrily, "Hanuman, everyone including Karna will die if you glare at him like that. Please sit quietly on Arjuna's flagstaff." As Hanuman calmed down, Krishna said gently, "Karna is fated to die at the hands of Arjuna. Besides, he is the son of your Guru, Suryadev and you cannot kill him." Hanuman obeyed Krishna quietly.

314 Hanuman the Protector

During the war, Krishna would applaud Karna each time his arrow hit Arjuna's chariot. But he never praised Arjuna's skills. A disheartened Arjuna questioned Krishna about this. "Your chariot is protected by Hanuman. But Karna's chariot is not protected by anyone which demands applause," Krishna replied. When the war ended, and Hanuman and Krishna left, Arjuna's chariot caught fire and was reduced to ashes. "Arjuna, your chariot was destroyed by Karna a long time ago. It was only functioning because Hanuman was perched on your flag and I was protecting it," Krishna explained.

315 Balarama's Ego

After killing the mighty demon Dwiti, Balarama had become vain. Wanting to rid Balarama of his vanity, Krishna decided to seek Hanuman's help who was the only one strong enough for direct combat with Balarama. Krishna hatched a plot with Narada who went to Hanuman and asked him if he had heard of Balarama who claimed to be even more powerful than Lord Rama. "There is no one who is stronger than Lord Rama," Hanuman insisted angrily. He was also angered because of the name 'Balarama'. "If he does not change his name, I shall destroy him," he declared.

316 Hanuman in Balarama Vatika

Hanuman was furious to know about Balarama. "How dare he keep a name like that and claim to be greater than Lord Rama? Ask him to change his name immediately. He shall have to face me in battle otherwise," Hanuman thundered. Narada said, "Many people including Lord Krishna himself have tried to explain this to him. But Balarama just doesn't listen." Hanuman decided to teach him a lesson.

Disguised as an ordinary monkey, Hanuman entered the Balarama Vatika. He started eating the fruits and destroying the garden. Balarama's soldiers tried to chase him away but failed. "Capture that monkey!" Balarama angrily ordered his commander.

317 Hanuman Tricks Balarama

Balarama's commander tried to shoot down the monkey. Hanuman descended from the tree, slapped the commander hard and snatched away his bow to break it. The commander fled to Balarama. "This is not an ordinary monkey, but a demon in disguise," he exclaimed fearfully. Balarama angrily strode towards the garden to destroy the demon.The monkey continued plundering the garden. Balarama used all his weapons to capture him but failed.

"O Vanara!" he shouted angrily, his ego shattered. "I know you are no ordinary monkey. Whoever you are, reveal your identity at once or I shall hurl my plough at you."

318 Balarama's Pride Broken

Balarama threatened to throw his weapon, the plough, at Hanuman when he realised he had been tricked. Hanuman knew that he was immune to all weapons but did not want to insult Balarama as he had learnt his lesson. Hanuman prayed to Lord Krishna to rescue him from this dilemma. Krishna appeared immediately and halted Time to reveal himself to Balarama and Hanuman in his Vishwaroopam or the ultimate form of Vishnu. Balarama immediately laid down his weapon and bowed before Mahavishnu. Hanuman did the same.

Lord Vishnu said to Balarama. "This monkey is none other than the mighty Hanuman whom I had sent to remove your ego." Hanuman and Balarama embraced each other lovingly.

319 Hanuman Protects Vaishno Devi

Vaishno Devi, an incarnation of Goddess Durga, once went to Trikuta hill to pray. An evil demon Bhairavnath wanted to abduct her. But Hanuman got to know about the demon's plan. He flew to Trikuta hill to protect her. Vaishno Devi began meditating in a cave. Hanuman guarded the cave for nine months till the meditation continued. During this period he fought fierce battles with the demon to keep him away from the cave.Finally, defeated by Hanuman, Bhairavnath fled to the nearby forest. Goddess Vaishno Devi emerged from the cave after nine months and thanked Hanuman who was thirsty. To quench his thirst, the goddess shot an arrow into the Earth to bring forth a stream of water which is known as Banganga today. A dip in this holy river is believed to work miracles.

320 The Legend of the Jagannath temple

The southern entrance of the Jagannath temple of Puri is named Hanumandwaar or 'The Gate of Hanuman'. Hanuman once arrived in this temple for Lord Jagannath's darshan. Suddenly, a terrible storm broke out threatening to destroy the temple. The devotees were disturbed by the loud roar of the ocean which reached the inside of the temple to disturb their prayers. Hanuman bound the ocean in chains and tamed the storm. The temple was saved. But he got entangled in the chains that had Lord Rama's name written on them. Lord Jagannath then appeared in the dreams of his chief devotees and asked them to tie Hanuman to the temple door with those very chains, to always protect the temple with his presence. It is believed that Hanuman stays in the temple now, inside which the ocean is scared to roar.

321 Tulsidas and the Preta

Tulsidas, a great devotee of Lord Rama and Hanuman, lived in the 15th century. He wrote the 'Ramcharitmanas' and the 'Hanuman Chalisa'. He would go to the woods outside Varanasi for his morning ablutions. He carried his water pot with him for his prayers, and on the way back home would offer the remaining water to a tree in the woods. A preta lived in this tree. Tulsidas's regular offering of water quenched the thirst of this spirit. Pleased, it appeared beforeTulsidas and said, "You have quenched my thirst. Ask me for any boon and it shall be granted." Tulsidas replied, "My only wish is to meet Lord Rama once in my lifetime."

322 Tulsidas's Wish

Tulsidas asked the preta to grant him the boon of Lord Rama's Darshan. The preta exclaimed, "This is something beyond my powers. Ask for wealth, power or anything else, and I shall grant it to you. But to reach Lord Rama is impossible." But Tulsidas did want anything else in this life or the next, but to meet Lord Rama.

The preta said that he could guide him to Rama's greatest devotee, Hanuman. "If you manage to convince Hanuman, he might make you meet Lord Rama." Tulsidas was very pleased. The preta revealed, "Hanuman is the first one to come to the Rama temple every evening to listen to the Ramkatha, disguised as an old leper. Everyone stays away from him."

323 Tulsidas Meets Hanuman

Following the preta's advise, Tulsidas visited the temple. The first visitor was indeed a leper who took his place at the end of the gathering and sat there quietly till the Ramkatha was over. Then, he left and Tulsidas followed him. At an isolated spot, he fell at the leper's feet. "I know who you are, My Lord," he exclaimed. The leper tried to convince him that he was mistaking him for someone else. But Tulsidas would not give in as he held the leper's feet and cried. Moved, the leper assumed his original form of Hanuman to bless Tulsidas. Tulsidas wept tears of joy. "My only wish is to meet Lord Rama," he said humbly. "Please help me!" Seeing Tulsidas's devotion, Lord Vishnu took Rama's form and met him to grant his wish.

324 Akbar Imprisons Tulsidas

The news of Tulsidas meeting Lord Rama reached Mughal Emperor Akbar who summoned him to his court and challenged him to show Lord Rama to him. "One cannot meet Lord Rama without true devotion," Tulsidas replied. Akbar ordered Tulsidas to write some couplets in his praise. When Tulsidas refused, Akbar ordered to throw him into the dungeon. Tulsidas kept chanting Lord Rama's name. He wrote the beautiful verses of the Hanuman Chalisa in this prison. After Tulsidas completed writing the Hanuman Chalisa as an ode to Hanuman, an army of monkeys entered Delhi and plundered shops and harassed people. Akbar's mighty Mughal army could not control this monkey army. Akbar was forced to release Tulsidas and the monkeys stopped their mischief and disappeared miraculously.

325 The Karmanghat Hanuman Temple

The 12th century Karmanghat Hanuman Temple in Hyderabad has an interesting legend. Once, while hunting in the forest, a Kakatiya king felt tired. As he sat down to rest under the shade of a tree, he heard someone chanting Lord Rama's name. The source of the sound led him deeper into the forest where he discovered a stone idol of Hanuman in a sitting posture. The king realised that the chants were emerging from this idol. The king shared the news of this miracle with his close ones. That night, Lord Hanuman appeared in the king's dream and asked him to construct a temple. The king ordered the construction of the Karmanghat Temple immediately and the succeeding kings of the Kakatiya dynasty ensured that the temple was well maintained.

326 Karmanghat Protected

Four hundred years later, the Karmanghat Hanuman Temple was threatened with demolition when the Mughal Emperor Aurangzeb ordered his armies to demolish all major Hindu temples throughout the country. When Aurangzeb's army arrived to destroy the temple, they discovered that a strange force did not allow them to enter the compound walls of this temple. Aurangzeb decided to destroy the temple himself. Armed with a crow bar held threateningly in his hand, Aurangzeb arrived at the temple. As he raised the crow bar to strike at the temple walls, there was a deafening roar that emerged from within the temple. The crow bar slipped and fell from Aurangzeb's hand and a strange fear took over his senses.

"Mandir todna hai raja, to kar maan ghat," a powerful divine voice resonated. What it meant was- Oh king, if you want to destroy this temple, then first make your heart strong!

But Aurangzeb's heart was no longer strong. He abandoned his plan and fled from the temple which derived its name Karmanghat from the divine voice, and exists till date.

327 The Saint and the Lawyer

A sadhu used to beautifully narrate the Ramayana Katha. But he began his Ram Katha with a strange ritual that surprised many. Every day, before beginning his discourse, the sadhu would fold his hands pointing towards a particular direction and say, "Please take a seat, O mighty Bajrangbali." After inviting Hanuman, he would begin his discourse that lasted an hour. People whispered among themselves that the sadhu was hallucinating, but no one complained as his narration was superb and worth experiencing. One day, a famous lawyer arrived to listen to the sadhu. *Does the saint want us to believe that Lord Hanuman is present among us now?* he thought.

328 The Lawyer's Challenge

The lawyer challenged the sadhu. "Do you think that Lord Hanuman actually comes when you invite him to take a seat before you?" he asked the sadhu. The sadhu replied. "This is my personal belief that Lord Hanuman is present when I'm reciting the Rama Katha." The lawyer laughed. "You have to prove to us that Lord Hanuman comes to listen to your Katha and is really here."

"Never put one's devotion on the weighing scales of evidence," the sadhu replied, "This is a matter between god and his devotee's love." But the lawyer was hellbent on his request and also gathered the support of a few locals. "You must show us Lord Hanuman's presence as you claim," he insisted.

329 Challenge Accepted

The sadhu accepted the lawyer's challenge and agreed to show him Hanuman's presence the very next day before he began his Katha. The lawyer thought happily, *The sadhu's false claim will be exposed before his devotees.* The sadhu handed a cushion to the lawyer. "This is the cushion on which I request Lord Hanuman to sit every day," he said. "Take it with you and bring it tomorrow." The lawyer returned with it the next day. The news about the challenge had spread across the land and there was a huge crowd to witness it.

The sadhu asked the lawyer what he would do if he was defeated. "I shall give up my practice as a lawyer and become your disciple," the lawyer replied. "What will you do if you are defeated?" "I shall stop my religious discourses and become your servant " the sadhu replied.

330 The Miracle

People watched with bated breath as the challenge began. "After I invite Lord Hanuman to take his seat, hold up the cushion high in the air," the sadhu said to the lawyer. "If you manage to lift the cushion, you will have won as it will mean that Lord Hanuman is not present on the seat." The sadhu folded his hands and tearfully invited Lord Hanuman to join the gathering and take his seat on the cushion. "I am your simple devotee, My Lord," he prayed. "Please accept my invitation and save my honour." Then, the sadhu invited the lawyer to lift the cushion.

The lawyer tried to lift the cushion. He pulled with all his might but the cushion refused to budge. Finally, the lawyer fell at the sadhu's feet, sweating profusely. "Forgive me for doubting your devotion, O holy one," he said.

331 Hanuman Worshipped As a Woman

There is a unique 10,000 year old Hanuman temple in Chhattisgarh. The legend is that Prithvi, the king of Ratanpur contracted the dreaded leprosy for which there was no cure in those days. He prayed to Hanuman every day and asked him to cure him. One night, Hanuman appeared in his dream and asked him to construct a temple. "Take out the idol from Mahamaya Kund and establish it in the temple," Hanuman ordered. The next day, King Prithvi ordered his men to fish out the idol from the lake. But the idol was in the form of a woman as the lake belonged to Goddess Mahamaya. King Prithvi established the idol in the temple but as he was a devotee of Hanuman, it was Hanuman who was worshipped here in the form of a woman and the king was cured of his leprosy.

332 The Brahmin and His Wife

In a town named Rishinagar lived a rich, well respected brahmin named Keshavdutta. Every Tuesday, Keshavdutta and his wife fasted and prayed to Hanuman. But even after many years of fasting and prayers, they were not blessed with a child. They were disappointed but continued worshipping Hanuman. One day, Keshavdutta decided to go to the jungle and perform severe penance by praying to Hanuman to grant his wish. His wife prayed at home. One Tuesday, she fasted but couldn't go to the Hanuman temple to offer prayers. Out of guilt, she decided not to eat anything till next Tuesday till she had performed her prayers for Lord Hanuman.

333 Keshavdutta's Son Mangal

Keshavdutta's wife decided to fast for a week after missing her Tuesday worship of Hanuman and break her fast only after worshipping Hanuman the next Tuesday. But after offering prayers to Hanuman, she fainted out of hunger and exhaustion. Her neighbours carried her home and revived her. That night, Hanuman visited her in her dream. "I'm pleased with your devotion and prayers," Hanuman said. "I grant you the boon that you shall have a handsome and strong son!"

Soon, with Hanuman's blessings, she gave birth to a son whom she named Mangalprasad because he was born on a Tuesday. Keshavdutta returned home after a few days and was surprised to see Mangal. "Whose son is this?" he asked suspiciously. His wife told him about Hanuman's visit in her dream and how he had given her the boon of a son. But Keshavdutta didn't believe her.

334 Hanuman Saves Mangal

Keshavdutta didn't believe that Mangal was his son and was suspicious of his wife. *She has betrayed me*, he thought. *Now she's lying to me to hide her sins*. He decided to kill Mangal. One day, while going to the well to bathe, Keshavdutta took Mangal along. He threw him inside the well and returned home.

"Have you seen Mangal ? "His wife asked him. He lied and said he hadn't. That very moment, the toddler Mangal came walking towards them. Keshavdutta was stunned. *How is this possible*? he thought. That night, Keshavdutta saw Hanuman in his dream. "Why are you trying to kill your own child?" Hanuman scolded Keshavdutta. "How can you doubt such a pious and loving wife? I had given your wife the boon of having a son. I have saved your son's life. But the next time you try to do something foolish, I shall ensure that you end up in the well yourself!" Keshavdutta woke up in a sweat and apologised to his wife. From that day onwards, he loved Mangal dearly.

335 Hanuman Worship Banned in Village

Hanuman is worshipped throughout the length and breadth of India. In every town or village, one sees a temple or a small idol of Hanuman. But there lies a small village named Drongiri in Uttarakhand where Hanuman is not worshipped. Not only that, the red colour which is so symbolic with Hanuman is also banned in this village. This practice has been followed for centuries. Hanuman had uprooted the Drongiri Mountain which stood near this village to carry to Lanka with the Sanjeevani herb to revive Lakshmana. The villagers of Drongiri consider the Drongiri Mountain as god and still pray to it. They are of the opinion that when Hanuman uprooted this holy mountain it was deep in meditation. Hanuman not only broke the mountain's penance but also did not seek its permission to take the Sanjeevani herb, or to uproot it.

The villagers also do not plant red flags in their village as a tribute to the mountain that they believe is bleeding till today because of Hanuman's act. That is the reason why Hanuman is not worshipped in the village of Drongiri from Treta Yuga till today.

336 Hanuman Tests Macchindranath

Hanuman had fought many battles to emerge victorious. However, once, even Hanuman had to concede defeat in battle. The person who defeated Hanuman was also a devotee of Rama. Macchindranath was a great and powerful sage. He visited Rameshwaram once and after taking a dip in the ocean, the sage began praying to Lord Rama by standing in the ocean. Hanuman saw the great sage. He had heard great things about the devotion of Macchindranath. *Let me test the great sage's powers,* Hanuman thought. Using his yogic powers, Hanuman brought about rainfall in the area. It began to rain heavily but an unperturbed Macchindranath continued praying.

Let me attract the sage's attention, Hanuman thought, as his efforts to disturb the sage's meditation failed. Hanuman assumed the form of an ordinary monkey and pretended to make a cave in the mountain next to the ocean to protect himself from the rain. As he did so, a few rocks plunged into the ocean to break Macchindranath's concentration. He opened his eyes and saw the monkey trying to create a shelter for himself.

337 Hanuman's Challenge

Macchindranath was irritated when his concentration was broken and he saw the monkey breaking the rocks in the mountain to create a shelter from the rain. "One does not dig a well when one is thirsty. You should have built a shelter for yourself earlier instead of starting when the rain began to fall," the sage chided. "Who are you to give me such advice?" Hanuman asked. "I am a Siddha Yogi blessed with the power of all the mantras," Macchindranath replied.

"What I know is that Lord Rama and Mahabali Hanuman are the most powerful beings on Earth," Hanuman said. "I have had the good fortune of serving them and they have given me a percentage of their powers. If you defeat me in battle, I shall believe your claim to be a Siddha Yogi and bow to you," Hanuman challenged the sage. Macchindranath accepted the challenge and soon a great battle began between two of Rama's great devotees.

338 Hanuman Defeated

Hanuman threw huge boulders at Macchindranath who stopped them easily. Then Hanuman uprooted seven mountains and threw them together at the sage. The sage closed his eyes and chanted divine mantras. The mountains reversed their paths to return to their original place. Hanuman uprooted the largest mountain and held it above his head.

This is no ordinary monkey, the sage thought, and picked up a few drops of water from the ocean on his palm. Using his Vatakarshan mantra, he flung the water towards Hanuman. As soon as the water touched Hanuman's body, he stood still as a statue. The power of the sage's mantra also weakened Hanuman's power and he struggled under the huge weight of the mountain. Seeing his son struggle, Vayu appeared before Macchindranath and requested him to forgive Hanuman. The surprised sage immediately freed Hanuman who bowed before him and apologised. The sage forgave him.

339 Shani Becomes a Woman

The temple of Shanidev at a village named Sarangpur in Bhavnagar, Gujarat, features Shani as a woman. There is an interesting story behind this idol. Once, Lord Shani began to trouble the humans. Devotees of Hanuman were aware that only Hanuman could save them from Shani's ill effects and prayed to him.

Shani has broken his promise of not troubling my devotees, Hanuman thought angrily, and decided to beat him with his mace. When Shani became aware that Hanuman was looking for him, he was greatly alarmed. He ran for his life but Hanuman followed him everywhere. Finally, when Hanuman came face to face with Shani, the latter assumed the form of a woman. *Being a Brahmachari and someone who respects women, Hanuman will never lift a hand on a woman*, Shani thought. Shani fell at his feet to ask for forgiveness. "I shall let you go this time," Hanuman warned Shanidev. "But remember your promise of never harming my devotees again!"

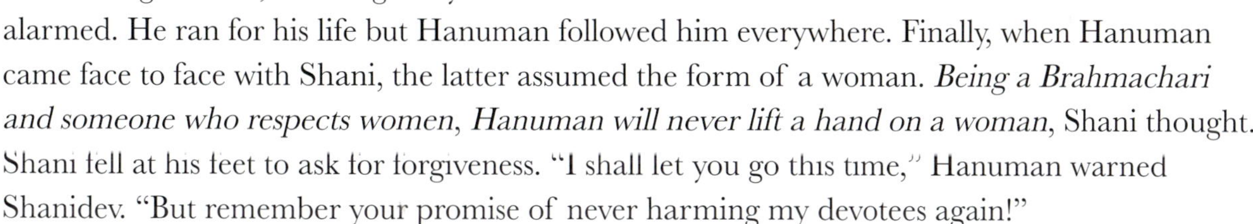

340 Friends of Hanuman

Rama's army had many valiant warriors apart from Hanuman. This was why they could defeat Ravana's army and win the war in just ten days. The king of the monkeys, Sugreev headed a force of over 10,00,000 monkeys. The army of bears was headed by the old and wise Jambavan, Rama's trusted advisor and an expert in setting up tents and camps, apart from his warfare skills. Other than Hanuman, Sugreev, Jambavan and Angad, there were some other brave warriors in Rama's army who were all friends and associates of the great Hanuman. The brothers Nal and Neel were warriors cum engineers and supervised the construction of the bridge to Lanka. Shatabali and Dwivid were great monkey warriors with thousands of elephants. Hanuman's father Kesari was another braveheart in this war, leading his monkey army of more than 1,00,000 warriors.

Although Hanuman eclipsed them all in bravery, they too were instrumental in Rama defeating Ravana

341 Hanuman's Longest Jumps

Hanuman used his two siddhis to expand and contract his form. But his jumps were unparalleled.

Hanuman made his longest jump in his childhood when he travelled all the way to the Sun, to eat it mistaking it for a fruit. The second amazing jump was when Hanuman leapt over the ocean to reach Lanka. The third jump was to get the Sanjeevani herb from the Drongiri Mountain to revive Lakshmana. The fourth long jump by Hanuman was when he went to rescue Rama and Lakshmana from Ravana's brother, Mahiravan in Pataal Lok. Hanuman's fifth amazing jump was in great joy, after Rama's coronation.

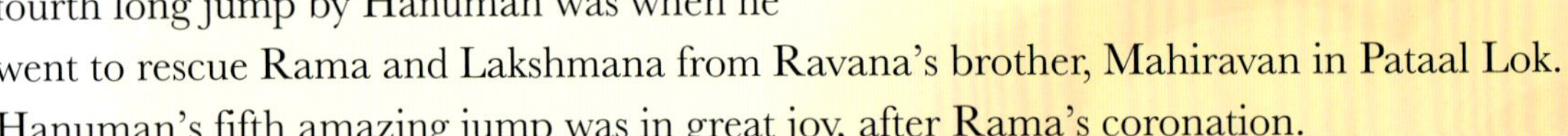

342 The Hanuman Chalisa

When he was imprisoned by the Mughal Emperor Akbar, Saint Tulsidas, the author of 'Ramcharitmanas' wrote the Hanuman Chalisa, a collection of 40 verses that tell the story of the devotion and submission of Hanuman to Lord Rama. He sang it for forty days in prison. Tulsidas says in the Hanuman Chalisa that whoever chants it with full devotion to Hanuman will have his blessings. This was proved true when after the 40-day chanting by Tulsidas, an army of monkeys invaded Delhi causing major problems for the citizens and Akbar was forced to free Tulsidas.

343 The Power of the Hanuman Chalisa

The Hanuman Chalisa is a symbol of strength. It highlights Hanuman's acts of devotion, bravery and selflessness. It is believed to invoke Hanuman's divine intervention to fight evil forces. Millions of devotees chant the Hanuman Chalisa every day and vouch for its effectiveness in protecting from harm.

Amazingly, Tulsidas also mentioned the approximate distance between the Sun and the Earth in the Hanuman Chalisa as early as the 15th century. It took scientists as long as the 17th century to do the same.

344 Yudhishthira's Rajasuya Yajna

Once Narada arrived before Yudhishthira the king of Hastinapura and said, "You must perform the Rajasuya Yajna which was your father's unfulfilled wish so that his soul is at peace." Yudhishthira agreed.

"You must invite Rishi PurushMriga, a great devotee of Lord Shiva and seek his blessings so that your Rajasuya Yajna is successful," Narada advised Yudhishthira. Rishi PurushMriga's upper body was of a man and the lower body was that of a deer. It was impossible to catch him as he ran with great speed when someone approached him.

345 Hanuman's Hair

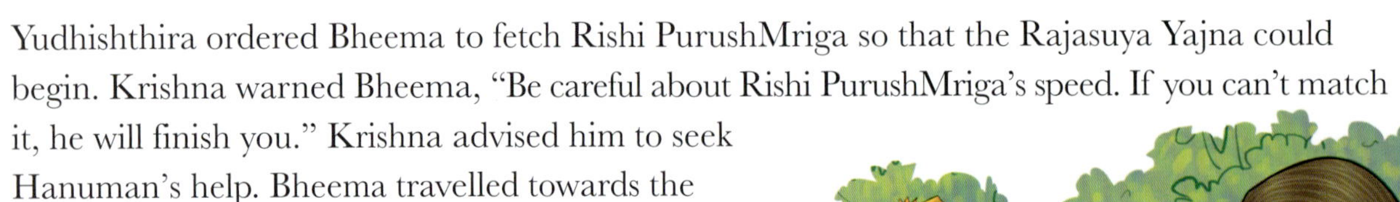

Yudhishthira ordered Bheema to fetch Rishi PurushMriga so that the Rajasuya Yajna could begin. Krishna warned Bheema, "Be careful about Rishi PurushMriga's speed. If you can't match it, he will finish you." Krishna advised him to seek Hanuman's help. Bheema travelled towards the Himalayas, and prayed to Hanuman after entering the forest. Bheema told him about the problem, and Hanuman suggested, "As Rishi PurushMriga is a devotee of Lord Shiva, you can check his speed by building Shivlings in his path. He is sure to stop and worship the Shivlings and that will check his progress."

346 Hanuman's Advice to Bheema

Hanuman plucked three hairs from his body and handed it to Bheema ."Each hair is blessed with the power of a thousand Shivlings," Hanuman explained. "When the sage tries to catch you, drop one hair on the ground and it will be converted into a thousand Shivlings. As the sage starts worshipping them, run as fast as you can. When he catches you again, do the same. These three hairs should help you beat him in the race to Hastinapura."

Bheema arrived at the hermitage where he saw the sage worshipping Lord Shiva.

347 The Sage's Condition

Bheema bowed before Rishi PurushMriga, who opened his eyes.

"O holy one," Bheema said respectfully. "I am the second Pandava, Bheema. I have come to invite you to Hastinapura on behalf of my elder brother, King Yudhishthira to bless us before the Rajasuya Yajna."

"I shall come with you on one condition," the sage declared. "You have to reach Hastinapura before I do. If you fail to do so, I shall kill you."

Bheema agreed as he had promised Yudhishthira that he would get the sage to Hastinapura. As soon as the condition was agreed upon, Bheema turned and ran with all his might. After running a fair distance, Bheema looked over his back to see if the sage was following him. To his surprise, he saw that Rishi PurushMriga was about to catch him. Recalling Hanuman's advice, Bheema instantly dropped one hair on the ground. As soon as he had done so, the hair was transformed into a thousand Shivlings. Bheema saw the sage sit down and begin worshipping Lord Shiva. He ran like the wind.

348 The Great Race

As Rishi PurushMriga was a die-hard devotee of Lord Shiva, he kept praying to the thousand Shivlings that formed miraculously after Bheema dropped Hanuman's hair on the ground. But Rishi PurushMriga finished his worship and caught up with Bheema because of his deer-like swiftness. His lower body was that of a deer and there was no way Bheema could beat him in speed. Bheema was close to Hastinapura when the sage caught up with him for the third time. After dropping the last hair and running away as the sage worshipped the Shivlings, Bheema was worried.

I have to run faster if I have to beat this sage. I shall reach Hastinapura which is only a few miles ahead, Bheema thought, and ran for his life. He was relieved when he spotted the gate of Hastinapura and ran towards it. Just then, he heard a roar and saw Rishi PurushMriga right behind him. Just as Bheema was about to enter the gate, the sage grabbed Bheema from behind. Bheema took a mighty leap towards the gate.

349 Fair Justice

As Rishi PurushMriga grabbed Bheema in a stronghold from behind, Bheema landed inside the gate but his feet remained outside. "I have beaten you!" the sage exclaimed. "Now, I shall kill you." Bheema argued that he was inside the gate. A fierce argument broke out between them. Krishna and Yudhishthira quickly arrived to separate them. The rishi beseeched Yudhishthira to solve the dispute. "Bheema's legs are still outside the gate, so they belong to Rishi PurushMriga," Yudhishthira declared. Pleased with Yudhishthira's justice, the sage spared Bheema. He participated in the Rajasuya Yajna and blessed the Pandavas.

350 The Legend of Siddhabali

Hanuman had granted permission to his devotee, a great sage, to marry. This displeased the sage's disciple Guru Goraknath. He decided to free his guru from domestic life. While crossing a forest, Hanuman appeared in the guise of a tribal and tried to stop him. A fierce battle broke out. Hanuman couldn't defeat Goraknath. Revealing his true form he told Goraknath to ask for a boon. Goraknath requested him to free his guru from domestic life and guard the temple that was supposed to be built in his name. Hanuman did not agree to the first request. However, he granted the second wish and watches over the Siddhabali Baba temple.

351 Slow Trains

The Hanuman temple in Bolai in Madhya Pradesh believed to be 600 years old has an unbelievable secret. This temple has an idol of Lord Ganesha placed to the left side of Hanuman's idol. Locals believe that having both gods in this temple makes it a special and lucky place.

But that doesn't explain the mysterious circumstances in which speeding trains automatically slow down while passing by this temple. There are many miracles that happen in this temple but this is the biggest miracle of them all. Train drivers have reported that they feel as if someone tells them to slow down when they are near the temple, and they do so even against their wishes. If a driver does not pay any heed to the mysterious voice, the train still slows down on its own. Even the railway officials are clueless about this strange incident. The priest of this temple has said that the trains slow down here automatically after an accident where two goods trains collided on the tracks near this temple.

352 The Miracle of Bandariya

Another miracle of Hanuman has been reported from a village named Bandariya which literally means 'female monkey'. The astonishing miracle is that this idol has kept growing in size over the years. Locals have claimed that this Hanuman idol was only 3 feet in size when it was first discovered in the village. Currently the Hanuman idol stands at a height of seven and a half feet. Because of this miraculous growth, people flock here from near and far. A few years ago, an attempt was made to steal this famous idol but the thieves failed in their attempt. Locals believe that if a true devotee prays in this temple on Hanuman Jayanti, all their prayers are answered.

353 Hanuman's Weapons

Besides the ability to fly, and transform his size, Hanuman's main weapons were the mace gifted by Lord Vishnu, with which he had destroyed Ravana's chariot in battle; Indra's Vajra, Lord Shiva's Shul, Pashupat and the Trishul. It is also said that Hanuman's left hand had the power of a mace. He also used his body parts as weapons. He fought with his fists and used his tail to capture enemy soldiers, or to burn down Lanka. He also uprooted mountains, boulders, rocks and trees and flung them at the enemy. Hanuman could also increase his form to a monstrous size to use his feet as weapons to trample the enemy.

354 The Busy King

A king was a devotee of Lord Rama but he never had time to pray. One day, Narada told him about the value of chanting the name of Lord Rama. The king told him how he was busy and had no time for worship. Narada knew that this was true. "Don't you have any spare time in your busy day?" Narada asked. "The only free time when I'm undisturbed is when I am in the bathroom," the king replied. Narada advised him to chant Rama's name there. The king started chanting Lord Rama's name everyday in the bathroom. One day, Hanuman heard about this king who was chanting Lord Rama's name in the bathroom and was angry.

355 Narada Explains to Hanuman

Hanuman was furious when he heard that the king chanted Lord Rama's name from an impure place. He arrived at the king's palace and tried to knock down the bathroom door as the king chanted Rama's name inside. But no matter how hard he tried, he couldn't break open the door. Suddenly, Narada appeared before him and said, "While chanting the holy name of Lord Rama, a devotee cannot be hurt as the Lord's grace is on him. Lord Rama's name is too strong to be contaminated in any place. The place doesn't matter as long as one is chanting devotedly." Hanuman realised his mistake and calmed down.

356 The Famous Five Sages

Other than Tulsidas and the two Pandavas, Bheema and Arjuna, five great sages have also received Hanuman's Darshan. Satya Sai Baba claimed to his devotees that he had met Hanuman. Madhavacharya, a great saint was a devotee of Lord Rama. He received a darshan from Hanuman in his ashram.Guru Ramdas had also received Hanuman's darshan. He was a great devotee of Hanuman and the Guru of Chhatrapati Shivaji, the great Maratha warrior king. He spread the devotion of Rama and Hanuman throughout Maharashtra and built akhadas in the Hanuman temples which trained warriors for the Maratha army. Raghavendra Swami was a revered Guru of the Madhav community. Many miracles are associated with his life. Hanuman's visit is one of them. Neem Karoli Baba, a great devotee of Hanuman had established many Hanuman temples. It is said that Hanuman visited him many times.

357 Hanuman and the Old Woman

An old woman was a great devotee of Hanuman and worshipped him every Tuesday. Hanuman decided to test her. He disguised himself as a sage and came outside her house. "Is there any devotee of Hanuman here who can fulfill my wish?" he shouted loudly. The old woman came out of her house and bowed before him. The sage demanded, "Serve me some food immediately." The old woman requested,"Please give me some time to cook the food." The angry sage said, "Go and fetch your son. I shall cook on his back." The terrified old lady fetched her son and the sage cooked food on his back. The old woman ran inside her house, crying. The sage followed her. "Call your son," he smiled. The woman did so and was surprised to see that her son was unhurt. The sage turned into Hanuman and blessed her.

358 The Temple of Hanuman and His Wife

Surya had nine divine Vidyas that he had to teach Hanuman but four of these Vidyas could only be learnt by a married person. Surya asked Hanuman to marry his daughter Suvarchala whom he created with the power of his divine rays. Lord Surya assured him, "Your vow of brahmacharya will be maintained. This marriage is only for you to learn the remaining Vidyas." Hanuman agreed. After the marriage, Suvarchala left to perform deep penance. Hanuman did not lose his brahmacharya.

A famous temple in Telangana worships Hanuman and his wife. This is the only temple of its kind. Devotees flock to see the idol of the married Hanuman. The day of Hanuman's marriage is celebrated in this temple amid great festivity.

359 Black-faced Hanuman

The idol of Hanuman in a temple in Rajasthan built by Aamer's Raja Jaisingh is black instead of the usual red, and is made of silver. A legend says that when Hanuman completed his studies, he asked Suryadev what Gurudakshina he should give him. Lord Surya revealed to Hanuman that his son Shani had left him and he wanted him back as Gurudakshina. Hanuman approached Shani and asked him to return to Lord Surya. There was a fierce fight in which Hanuman defeated Shanidev and led him back to Lord Surya. But in the fight, Shanidev burnt Hanuman's face and it turned black as depicted in this temple.

360 The Dejected Boy

Hanuman is worshipped by many sportspersons who believe that his blessings help them excel in sports. A young cricketer was a devotee of Hanuman. But he was sad because as a batsman he was not getting enough runs for his club. The coach had scolded him for his lack of form and commitment in front of the entire team. He dejectedly started walking home. On his way he visited a secluded Hanuman temple. A few devotees were praying. The boy joined them and started praying to Hanuman, telling him his troubles. When he opened his eyes, he saw that only he was left in the temple. Everyone else had left.

361 The Voice From the Idol

The boy saw a small stone outside this temple. *I am as useless as this stone*, he thought. "I know how you feel, my boy. I lay here on the ground for centuries. Nobody looked at me or cared for me," a voice said suddenly. He was startled. Was it the stone speaking or was it his imagination? It appeared that the stone was actually speaking to him."One day, a sculptor saw me and broke me into two pieces," the stone continued. "He used the bigger half to create the idol of Hanuman and left me, the smaller half here. Look how the idol is honoured and how I am still neglected. Is it fair?"

The boy saw the decorated idol of Hanuman inside the temple and felt sorry for the poor stone lying outside. "I have earned this honour," a voice emerged from the idol. *Is Hanumanji speaking now?* the boy wondered.

362 No Pains, No Gains

The boy realised that the idol was addressing the smaller stone. "The sculptor hammered me with his tools and it was so painful," the voice said. "But I bore all the pain to become an idol. As I cried in pain, you were happy that you had been spared by the sculptor. You cannot achieve anything unless you bear the kind of hammering that I received. That's why I'm worshipped today, while you are not!"

The boy had just learnt an important lesson. *I must not take the coach's scolding to heart. I shall practice harder to improve my game. Hanumanji has answered my prayers*, he thought happily. The next day, he reported to his coach, ready to be hammered into shape as a good cricketer.

363 The Legend of the Jakhu Temple

The Jakhu temple of Hanuman in Shimla has a legend unlike any other. It is said that Hanuman rested on Jakhu Mountain before he flew to the Himalayas to get the Sanjeevani herb for the injured Lakshmana. When Hanuman arrived there with a band of monkeys, he met Rishi Yaku who gave useful information about the Sanjeevani herb. The band of monkeys remained there while Hanuman continued his journey. While returning, Hanuman could not stop at Jakhu Mountain because he had to return before sunrise to save Lakshmana. The sage built a temple in Hanuman's honour at the place where he had rested. The idol of Hanuman here is 108 feet high, and is one of the largest idols in India. A lot of monkeys are found here, as if awaiting Hanuman's return.

364 Famous Devotees of Hanuman

Chhatrapati Shivaji was a great devotee of Hanuman. He would hire soldiers from the Hanuman akhadas in the temples. He fought not only against the Mughals but also against other invaders. It is believed that Shivaji had the direct blessings of Hanuman who rescued him during many difficult situations in war. Shri Vyas Rai Teerth, was the Guru of Emperor Krishnadeva Raya. He persuaded the emperor to build as many as 732 Hanuman temples throughout India to spread devotion and train warrriors. He also authored great devotional books on Hanuman. The great Yogi, Swami Vivekananda was a disciple of Ramakrishna Paramhansa. Hanuman was his idol since childhood. Swami Vivekananda used to motivate his disciples by the examples of the heroics of Hanuman.

365 The Legend of Hanuman

Hanuman is a symbol of power and devotion. He is the only person to have served the two incarnations of Lord Vishnu - Lord Rama and Lord Krishna. Hanuman is a great Yogi who has transcended the five senses. In the Tamil Kamba Ramayanam, the significance of the number five is beautifully narrated:

Hanuman is the son of one of the five elements (son of the wind). He crossed one of the five elements (water – the ocean) through one of the five elements (the sky). He met the daughter of one of the five elements (Sita, daughter of Earth) and burnt down Lanka by using one of the five elements (Fire).

He is the 'Sankat Mochan' or 'the one who relieves us from troubles'.

The scriptures say that Hanuman dwells in a farway cave chanting the name of Lord Rama and awaits his next incarnation.

Inspired by Hanuman's devotion, devotees in the Bala Hanuman Temple in Jamnagar, Gujarat, have been chanting Lord Rama's name continuously, and taking turns to chant night and day since 1 August 1964.

OTHER TITLES IN THIS SERIES

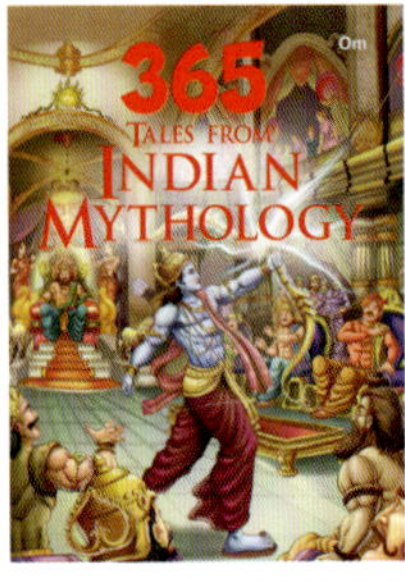

ISBN: 978-81-87107-46-0

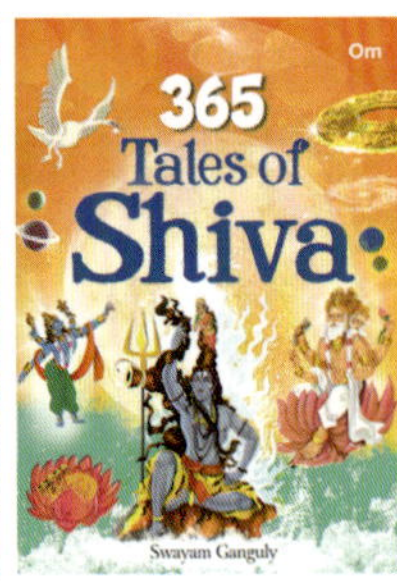

ISBN: 978-93-52767-22-9

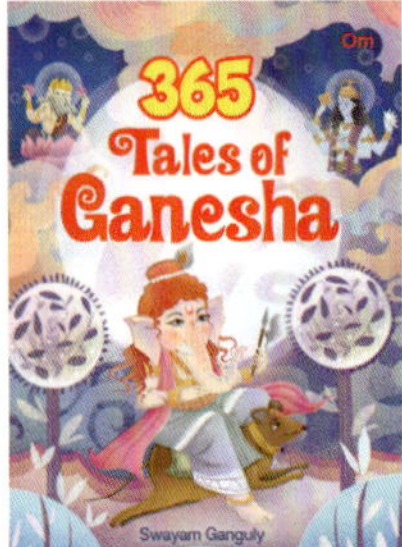

ISBN: 978-93-52768-62-2

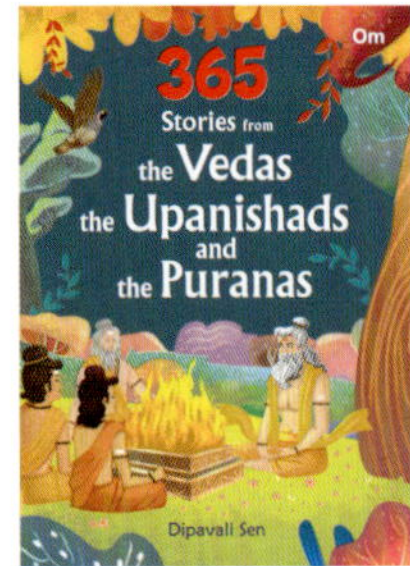

ISBN: 978-93-52768-64-6

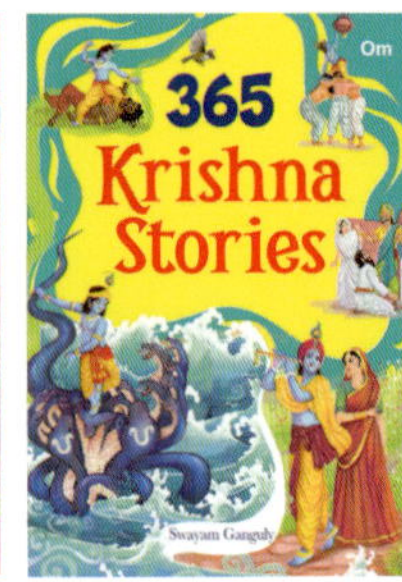

ISBN: 978-93-52767-23-6

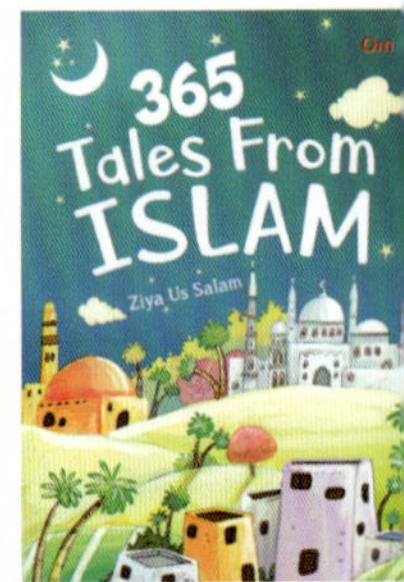

ISBN: 978-93-52764-05-

ISBN: 978-93-52760-96-1

ISBN: 978-93-85031-29-8

ISBN: 978-93-81607-49-7

ISBN: 978-93-83202-81-2

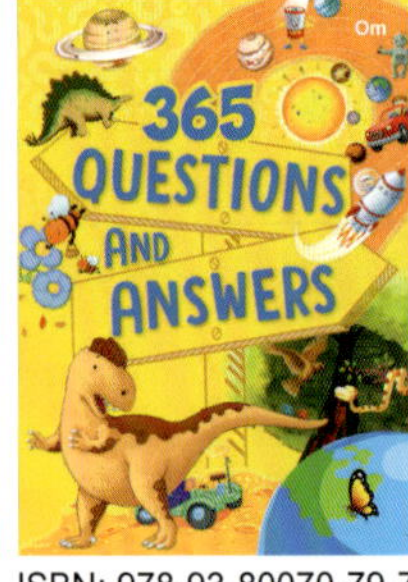

ISBN: 978-93-80070-79-7

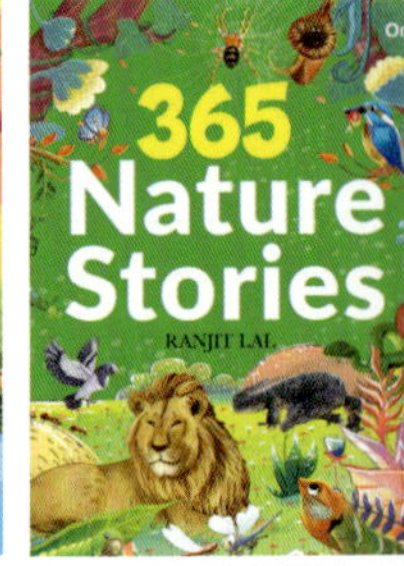

ISBN: 978-93-52764-06-

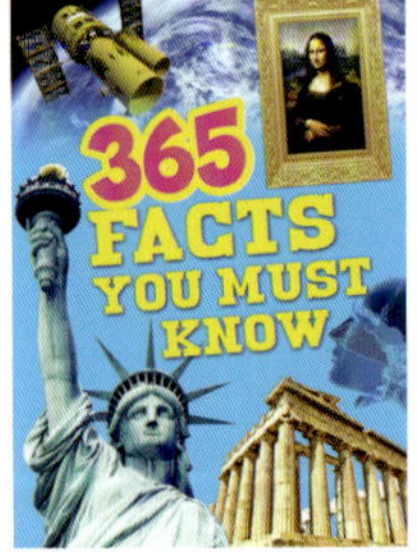

ISBN: 978-93-84225-33-9

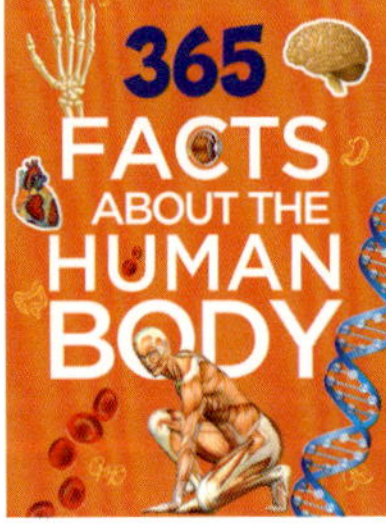

ISBN: 978-93-84625-93-1

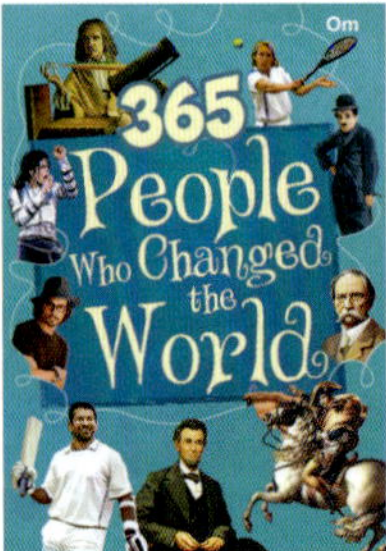

ISBN: 978-93-84225-34-6

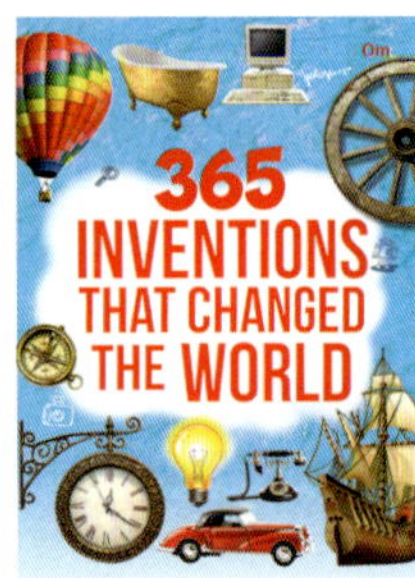

ISBN: 978-93-84625-92-4

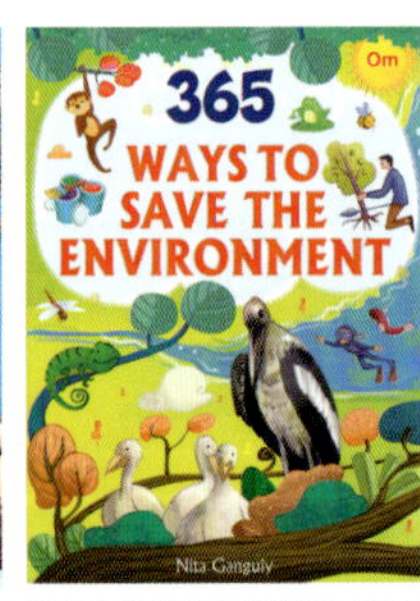

ISBN: 978-93-52760-95-4

ISBN: 978-93-80069-35-

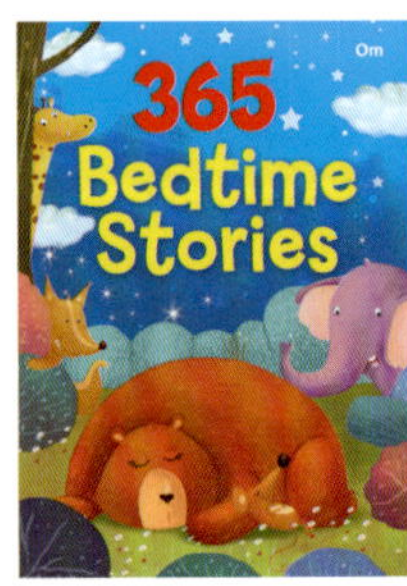

ISBN: 978-81-87107-53-8

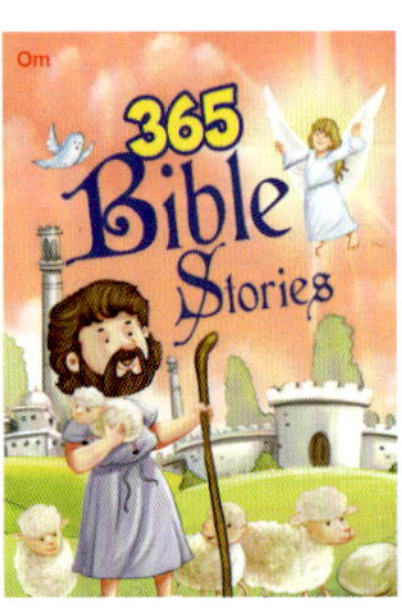

ISBN: 978-93-80069-36-4

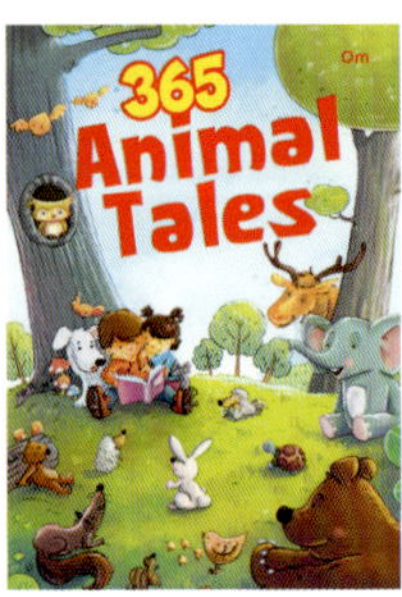

ISBN: 978-81-87107-52-1

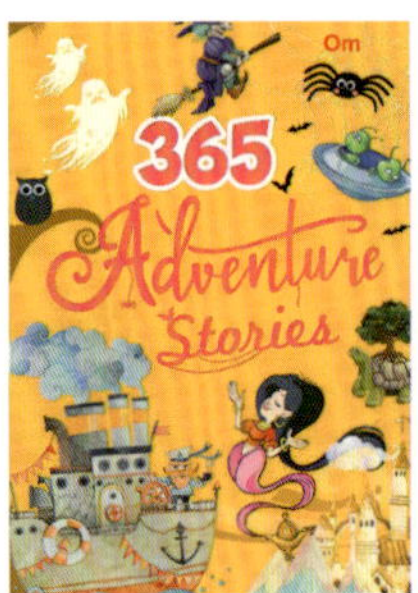

ISBN: 978-93-84225-32-2

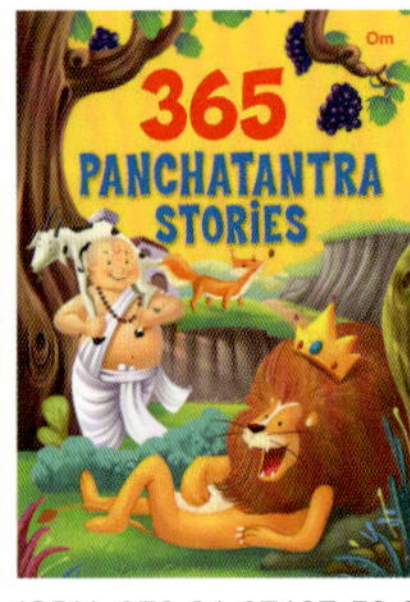

ISBN: 978-81-87107-58-3

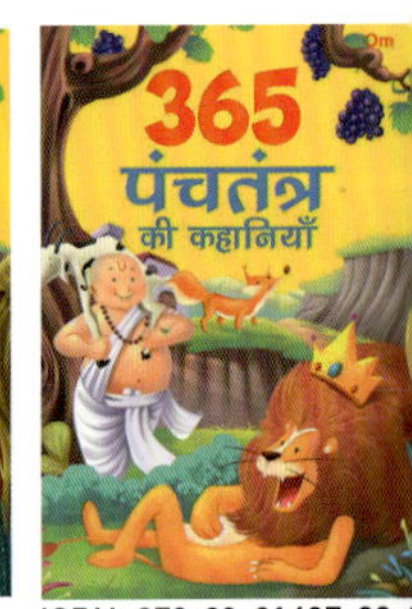

ISBN: 978-93-81607-80-(

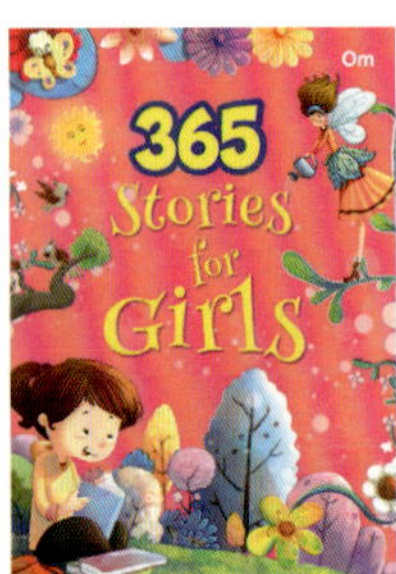

ISBN: 978-93-80070-84-1

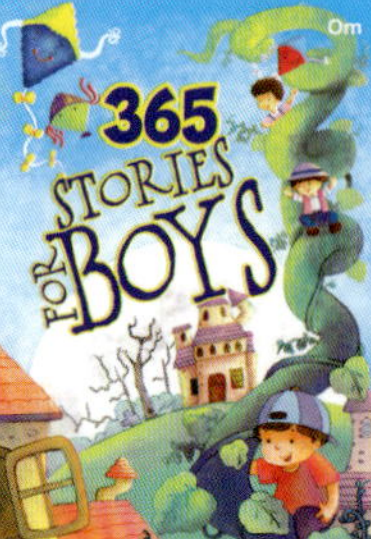

ISBN: 978-93-80070-83-4

365
GHOST
& HORROR
STORIES
Andaleeb Wajid

ISBN: 978-93-81607-57-2

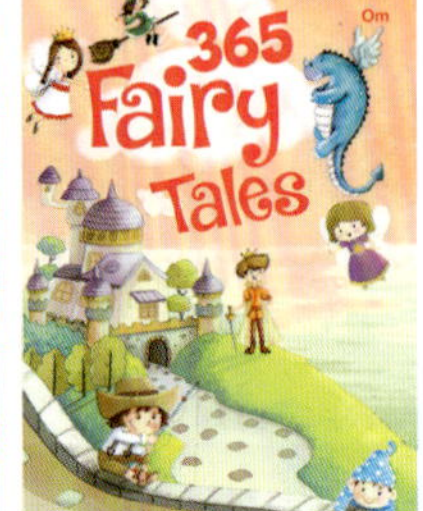

ISBN: 978-81-87107-55-2

365
Folk Tales

ISBN: 978-81-87107-56-9

ISBN: 978-93-84225-31